THAILAND UNVEILED :A
PREPARATION GUIDE

TOMAS GRAY

TABLE OF CONTENTS

CHAPTER 1:Introduction

1.1. Welcome to the Land of Smiles: Thailand

Thailand, known as the "Land of Smiles," is a captivating Southeast Asian gem that enchants travelers with its vibrant culture, rich history, stunning landscapes, and warm hospitality. This comprehensive travel guide invites you to embark on a journey through Thailand, exploring its diverse regions, traditions, and attractions that make it a truly remarkable destination.

The Heart of Thailand - Bangkok

The bustling capital city, Bangkok, is a sensory overload of sights, sounds, and flavors. From the majestic Grand Palace and intricate temples like Wat Pho with its iconic reclining Buddha, to the vibrant street markets and the energetic nightlife along Khao San Road, Bangkok is a city of contrasts that seamlessly blends tradition and modernity.

Ancient Kingdoms and Ruins

Venture north to the ancient city of Ayutthaya, a UNESCO World Heritage site, where you'll discover the remnants of a once-mighty kingdom. Explore the well-preserved temples and towering stupas that stand as a testament to Thailand's rich history.

Further north lies Sukhothai, another historical site with its own collection of temples and Buddha statues, offering a glimpse into Thailand's past.

Northern Charms - Chiang Mai and Beyond
Chiang Mai, nestled in the mountains, captivates with its laid-back atmosphere and artistic vibe. Explore its night markets, engage with local artisans, and partake in a traditional alms-giving ceremony. For the adventurous, the nearby hills offer trekking opportunities to hill tribe villages, providing a unique cultural experience.

Tropical Paradise - Southern Islands
Thailand's southern islands boast pristine beaches, crystal-clear waters, and a diverse marine life. Whether you choose the lively Phuket, the tranquil Phi Phi Islands, or the idyllic Krabi, each island offers its own brand of paradise. Snorkeling, diving, and island hopping are just a few of the activities that await.

Cultural Immersion - Chiang Rai and Isaan
Delve into the lesser-explored region of Isaan, where you'll find the city of Chiang Rai. Visit the famed White Temple (Wat Rong Khun) with its intricate and unconventional design. Isaan also offers a chance to experience traditional Thai rural

life and taste authentic dishes that are unique to this region.

Festivals and Traditions
Thailand's calendar is punctuated by vibrant festivals that celebrate its religious, cultural, and agricultural heritage. Songkran, the Thai New Year, is marked by water fights and symbolizes the cleansing of the old year. Loy Krathong sees thousands of lanterns floating on waterways, illuminating the night sky. The Phi Ta Khon Ghost Festival showcases elaborate masks and lively processions.

Gastronomic Delights
Thai cuisine is a feast for the senses, with its balance of sweet, sour, spicy, and savory flavors. From the aromatic street food stalls offering Pad Thai and Som Tum to upscale restaurants serving royal Thai cuisine, every meal is an opportunity to indulge in the country's culinary artistry.

Spirituality and Temples
Thailand's spiritual heritage is evident in its numerous temples and monasteries. Wat Arun's stunning spires and Wat Benchamabophit's marble architecture are just a couple of the many impressive sites. Travelers seeking spiritual

experiences can participate in meditation retreats or join monks for morning alms.

National Parks and Natural Wonders
For nature enthusiasts, Thailand's national parks are a treasure trove of biodiversity. Khao Sok National Park boasts lush rainforests, limestone cliffs, and the stunning Cheow Lan Lake. In the north, Doi Inthanon offers breathtaking vistas and the chance to spot rare bird species.

Etiquette and Cultural Sensitivity
Respecting Thai customs and traditions is crucial for a meaningful travel experience. Learn about the art of the wai, remove your shoes before entering temples, and dress modestly when appropriate. Thais value politeness, and a smile can go a long way in bridging cultural gaps.

Thailand is an exploration of a country that seamlessly blends ancient traditions with modern life. From the bustling streets of Bangkok to the tranquil beaches of the southern islands, from the spiritual havens of temples to the culinary delights of street vendors, Thailand offers a kaleidoscope of experiences that will leave an indelible mark on every traveler fortunate enough to visit. So pack your bags, immerse yourself in the vibrant tapestry of Thai culture, and prepare to be captivated by the Land of Smiles.

1.2. Why Thailand is Perfect for Children and Couples

Thailand, often referred to as the "Land of Smiles," is a versatile destination that caters to a wide range of travelers. From families with children seeking memorable experiences to couples in search of romance and adventure, Thailand offers a diverse array of attractions and activities that make it an ideal destination for both groups. In this guide, we'll delve into why Thailand is perfect for children and couples alike, exploring the unique experiences and opportunities it offers to create lasting memories.

Family-Friendly Adventures

Welcoming Culture
Thailand's renowned hospitality extends to families with children, creating a warm and inviting atmosphere. The locals' genuine fondness for children is evident in their interactions, making families feel at home even in the most exotic locations.

Beach Bliss
Thailand's pristine beaches are a playground for both kids and adults. From the calm waters of Phuket's Patong Beach to the natural beauty of Railay Beach in Krabi, families can enjoy building sandcastles, swimming, and participating in water sports together.

Elephant Encounters
A highlight for children is undoubtedly the opportunity to interact with elephants in ethical and responsible sanctuaries. These gentle giants provide an unforgettable experience as families feed, bathe, and learn about their conservation.

Kid-Friendly Attractions
Thailand's attractions cater to all ages. The Siam Ocean World in Bangkok offers an underwater adventure, while amusement parks like Dream World and Cartoon Network Amazone Waterpark provide endless fun for children.

Cultural Experiences
Exploring Thai culture with children can be both educational and entertaining. Visiting ancient temples like Wat Pho can be an opportunity for

learning and appreciating the history and artistry of Thailand.

Romantic Escapes for Couples

Idyllic Beach Retreats
Thailand's romantic allure is epitomized by its stunning beach resorts. The islands of Koh Phi Phi, Koh Lanta, and Koh Samui offer intimate settings with breathtaking sunsets, candlelit dinners on the sand, and moonlit walks.

Luxurious Spas
Couples seeking relaxation and rejuvenation will find a haven in Thailand's world-class spas. From traditional Thai massages to modern wellness treatments, these spas provide an opportunity for bonding and pampering.

Private Excursions
Thailand offers a range of private excursions for couples to explore its natural wonders. Kayak through the limestone caves of Phang Nga Bay or take a romantic sunset cruise along the Chao Phraya River in Bangkok.

Culinary Delights

Thailand's culinary scene is a feast for the senses, perfect for couples to savor together. From enjoying a candlelit dinner on a rooftop in Bangkok to taking a cooking class in Chiang Mai, the country's diverse cuisine enhances the romantic experience.

Adventure and Thrills

For couples seeking adventure, Thailand's diverse landscapes provide opportunities for activities like zip-lining through the jungle, snorkeling in crystal-clear waters, or exploring the lush rainforests.

The Best of Both Worlds

Family-Couple Balance

Thailand uniquely offers a blend of family-friendly and romantic experiences, making it an ideal destination for couples with children. Parents can enjoy moments of relaxation while kids engage in supervised activities, creating a harmonious balance.

Multigenerational Travel

Thailand's appeal extends beyond just couples and children. Grandparents, parents, and grandchildren can all find activities and attractions that cater to their interests, making it a perfect choice for multigenerational travel.

Unique Family Bonding
Family vacations in Thailand foster strong family bonds as everyone experiences new adventures together. Whether it's riding elephants, exploring ancient ruins, or simply enjoying local cuisine, shared experiences create lasting memories.

Couples Retreats
Even for families, Thailand offers opportunities for couples to enjoy romantic moments. Resorts often provide childcare services, allowing parents to have some alone time while children engage in supervised activities.

Thailand's allure for both children and couples is a testament to its diverse offerings and welcoming culture. Whether you're seeking a family adventure filled with cultural exploration and beach escapes or a romantic getaway with luxurious spas and intimate sunsets, Thailand caters to your desires. The Land of Smiles is indeed a versatile destination that provides the perfect canvas for creating cherished memories, no matter the composition of your travel party. So pack your bags, and let

Thailand enchant you with its blend of family-friendly fun and romantic allure.

CHAPTER 2: Essential Preparations

2.1. Traveling to Thailand: Tips and Tricks

Thailand, the captivating "Land of Smiles," is a dream destination that promises a rich tapestry of experiences. From vibrant cities to tranquil islands, from ancient temples to pristine beaches, the country has something for every traveler. To ensure your journey is seamless and rewarding, this guide offers essential tips and tricks for a successful adventure in Thailand.

Planning and Preparation

Visa Requirements
Before traveling, check the visa requirements for your nationality. Many nationalities can enter Thailand for tourism purposes without a visa for a specific duration, typically up to 30 days. If your stay exceeds this period, consider obtaining a visa in advance.

Travel Insurance
Invest in comprehensive travel insurance that covers medical expenses, trip cancellations, and unexpected incidents. This will provide peace of mind throughout your journey.

Vaccinations and Health Precautions

Consult your doctor for recommended vaccinations before traveling to Thailand. Carry prescription medications in their original packaging and be cautious with street food to prevent foodborne illnesses.

Packing Essentials

Clothing

Pack lightweight, breathable clothing suitable for Thailand's tropical climate. Modest attire is appropriate when visiting temples, so consider bringing long pants or skirts and covering your shoulders.

Sun Protection

Sunscreen, a wide-brimmed hat, sunglasses, and a reusable water bottle are essential to protect yourself from the strong tropical sun.

Insect Repellent

Thailand is home to mosquitoes, especially in certain regions. Carry insect repellent to avoid discomfort and reduce the risk of mosquito-borne illnesses.

Electronics

A universal power adapter, portable charger, and a waterproof phone case are valuable accessories. Consider bringing a camera to capture the beauty of Thailand's landscapes.

Cultural Etiquette

Respect for Religion

Thailand is deeply rooted in Buddhism, and temples are sacred spaces. Dress modestly, remove your shoes before entering, and refrain from showing public displays of affection within temple grounds.

Politeness and Gestures

The "wai" is a traditional Thai greeting involving a slight bow with palms pressed together. Return this gesture when appropriate, as it's a sign of respect.

Removing Shoes

Take off your shoes before entering homes, guesthouses, and some shops. This practice is a sign of cleanliness and respect for personal spaces.

Getting Around

Transportation Options
Thailand offers a variety of transportation options, from tuk-tuks and songthaews (shared trucks) to metered taxis and public buses. In cities like Bangkok, consider using the efficient Skytrain and subway systems.

Tuk-Tuk and Taxi Negotiations
Negotiate the fare before getting into a tuk-tuk or taxi. Insist on using the meter for taxis to avoid overcharging.

Renting Motorbikes
Renting a motorbike can be a convenient way to explore, but ensure you have a valid international driver's license and always wear a helmet.

Currency and Budgeting

Thai Baht (THB)
The official currency of Thailand is the Thai Baht. It's advisable to carry a mix of cash and credit/debit cards, as not all places accept cards, especially in rural areas.

Bargaining

Bargaining is common in markets and smaller shops. Be polite and willing to negotiate, but keep in mind that some prices are fixed.

Budgeting

Thailand offers options for all budgets. Accommodation, meals, and activities vary widely, so plan your budget according to your travel style.

Local Cuisine

Street Food

Thailand's street food is a culinary delight. Look for busy stalls with a steady stream of locals to ensure freshness and quality.

Spiciness

Thai cuisine can be spicy. If you're not accustomed to heat, request "mai ped" (not spicy) when ordering.

Water and Beverages

Stick to bottled water and avoid consuming ice in drinks from street vendors to prevent stomach issues.

Connectivity

SIM Cards
Purchase a local SIM card at the airport or convenience stores for affordable data and local calls. This will keep you connected throughout your trip.

Wi-Fi Availability
Many hotels, cafes, and restaurants offer free Wi-Fi, making it convenient to stay connected while exploring.

Language Basics

Common Phrases
Learning a few basic Thai phrases like "hello" (sawasdee) and "thank you" (kop khun) can go a long way in building rapport with locals.

Language Apps
Download language apps to help with communication and navigating local phrases.

Thailand's charm lies not only in its breathtaking landscapes and rich culture but also in its warmth and hospitality. By following these tips and tricks, you'll be better equipped to navigate the nuances of Thai travel, ensuring a seamless and enjoyable experience. Embrace the vibrant culture, savor the delectable cuisine, and immerse yourself in the diverse experiences that Thailand has to offer. With the right preparation, you're poised for an unforgettable journey in the Land of Smiles.

2.2. Packing Smart for a Family and Couple Adventure

Preparing for a family or couple adventure in Thailand requires thoughtful packing to ensure a comfortable and enjoyable journey. With a blend of cultural exploration, outdoor activities, and relaxation on the itinerary, strategic packing is key. This guide will help you pack smartly for your Thailand trip, considering the needs of both families and couples.

Family Packing Essentials

Clothing

Pack lightweight and breathable clothing suitable for Thailand's tropical climate. For children, consider clothing with sun protection features and hats. Modest attire is essential when visiting temples, so pack long pants or skirts and covering tops.

Footwear
Comfortable walking shoes are a must for everyone. Sandals and flip-flops are great for beach outings, while closed-toe shoes are suitable for urban exploration and hikes.

Baby and Toddler Gear
If traveling with young children, pack essential items such as diapers, wipes, formula, and baby food. A stroller and a baby carrier are invaluable for exploring and keeping little ones comfortable.

First Aid Kit
Include items like bandages, antiseptic ointment, pain relievers, and any prescription medications for family members.

Sun Protection
Pack sunscreen with high SPF, hats, and sunglasses to shield your family from the intense tropical sun.

Couple's Packing Essentials

Clothing

Opt for comfortable and versatile clothing suitable for warm weather. Include swimwear, lightweight tops, dresses, shorts, and a few evening outfits for romantic dinners.

Footwear

Comfortable walking shoes are essential for exploring, while dressier footwear is suitable for nights out. Don't forget flip-flops or sandals for the beach.

Travel Documents and Essentials

Carry passports, travel insurance details, and copies of important documents. A small daypack can hold essentials like a water bottle, sunscreen, and a camera.

Romantic Accessories

Consider packing a nice scarf, statement jewelry, or a tie for special evenings out.

Compact Toiletries

Opt for travel-sized toiletries or purchase items upon arrival. Include essentials like shampoo, conditioner, body wash, and skincare products.

Shared Packing Tips

Insect Repellent
Regardless of your travel group, insect repellent is crucial to avoid discomfort and prevent mosquito-borne illnesses.

Medications
Pack a small medical kit with basic medications like pain relievers, antacids, and motion sickness tablets. If someone in the group has allergies or specific medical needs, ensure you have the necessary supplies.

Universal Adapters
Thailand uses Type A, B, and C plugs, so a universal power adapter will ensure you can charge all your devices.

Portable Chargers
Keep your devices charged on the go with portable chargers, especially during long days of sightseeing.

Wet Wipes and Hand Sanitizer
Wet wipes are handy for quick cleanups, and hand sanitizer helps keep hands germ-free while traveling.

Reusable Water Bottles
Both families and couples can benefit from carrying reusable water bottles to stay hydrated throughout the day.

Packing smartly for a family or couple adventure in Thailand is essential to ensure a stress-free and enjoyable experience. Whether you're exploring ancient temples, relaxing on pristine beaches, or indulging in local cuisine, having the right essentials on hand will enhance your journey. By combining family-specific items and couple-specific necessities, you'll be well-prepared to embrace the wonders of Thailand with your loved ones. Remember that thoughtful packing allows you to fully immerse yourself in the beauty, culture, and adventure that the Land of Smiles has to offer.

2.3. Safety Guidelines for Children and Couples

Thailand's enchanting landscapes, vibrant culture, and warm hospitality make it an appealing destination for families and couples alike. While embarking on your adventure, prioritizing safety is crucial to ensure a memorable and worry-free experience. This guide provides comprehensive safety guidelines tailored to both children and couples, helping you navigate the diverse landscapes and experiences that Thailand has to offer.

Family Safety Guidelines

Supervision
When traveling with children, constant supervision is essential, especially in crowded places, near water, and during outdoor activities.

Health Precautions
Ensure your children are up to date with necessary vaccinations. Carry a basic first aid kit with items like bandages, antiseptics, and any necessary medications.

Safe Accommodation
Choose family-friendly accommodations that have safety features such as window locks, childproof outlets, and sturdy furniture.

Water Safety
While Thailand's beaches are beautiful, always be vigilant when swimming with children. Choose well-known and safe swimming spots, and keep a close eye on them at all times.

Safe Transportation

If using local transportation, such as tuk-tuks or songthaews, make sure they are safe and properly secured. If renting a car, use appropriate car seats for young children.

Couple Safety Guidelines

Travel Insurance

Invest in comprehensive travel insurance that covers medical emergencies, trip cancellations, and unexpected incidents.

Staying Together

In crowded places and unfamiliar areas, stay together as a couple. Avoid walking alone at night in poorly lit areas.

Alcohol Consumption

Moderate alcohol consumption is advisable. Be cautious when drinking in unfamiliar environments and always keep an eye on your drinks.

Safe Money Handling

Carry only necessary cash and use credit/debit cards whenever possible. Keep a record of your card details in a secure location.

Respect Local Customs

Understanding local customs and dressing modestly when appropriate helps couples blend in and minimizes unwanted attention.

Shared Safety Guidelines

Safe Exploration

Whether visiting bustling markets or serene temples, establish a meeting point in case you get separated. Share your itinerary and plans with a trusted friend or family member back home.

Scam Awareness

Be cautious of overly friendly strangers offering unsolicited advice or assistance. Research common scams to recognize and avoid them.

Food and Water Safety

Consume bottled water and eat at reputable establishments to reduce the risk of foodborne illnesses. Ensure street food is cooked properly.

Safe Adventures

When engaging in activities like trekking or water sports, choose reputable operators with safety equipment and experienced guides.

Emergency Contacts
Carry a list of emergency contacts, including local authorities, your country's embassy, and the contact information of your accommodations.

Safety is paramount when exploring the wonders of Thailand, whether as a family or a couple. By adhering to these comprehensive safety guidelines, you'll be better equipped to enjoy the diverse experiences the country has to offer while minimizing potential risks. Whether you're traversing bustling markets, relaxing on pristine beaches, or immersing yourselves in local culture, following these safety tips will ensure that your journey through the Land of Smiles is both enriching and secure. Remember, prioritizing safety allows you to fully embrace the beauty, culture, and adventure that make Thailand an unforgettable destination for families and couples alike.

CHAPTER 3: Exploring Thai Culture

3.1. Immerse Yourself in Thai Traditions and Customs

Thailand, the "Land of Smiles," is a country deeply rooted in rich traditions and cultural heritage. To truly experience the essence of Thailand, it's important to embrace its customs and traditions with respect and understanding. This guide provides comprehensive insights into Thai traditions, enabling you to engage with the local culture in a meaningful and respectful way.

The Wai - A Gesture of Respect

The Wai
The wai is a traditional Thai greeting that involves pressing the palms together in a prayer-like gesture and slightly bowing the head. This gesture is used to greet others, express gratitude, and show respect to elders or those of higher social status.

Proper Usage
When greeting someone, initiate the wai if they are of higher social standing or older than you. The height at which you hold your hands and the depth of your bow can vary depending on the context.

Returning the Wai

Return the wai with the same level of respect it was given to you. Children often wai by placing their hands at chest level, while adults might wai with their hands at forehead level.

Temple Etiquette

Dress Modestly

When visiting temples, dress conservatively by wearing clothes that cover your shoulders and knees. Removing your shoes before entering temple buildings is a sign of respect.

Proper Behavior

Inside temples, maintain a respectful and quiet demeanor. Refrain from pointing your feet at Buddha statues or images, as feet are considered the lowest part of the body.

Offering Alms

If you encounter monks during their morning alms rounds, you can offer food or donations. Approach respectfully and quietly, making your offering without direct physical contact.

Loy Krathong and Songkran Festivals

Loy Krathong
Loy Krathong, the "Festival of Lights," is celebrated by floating decorated baskets on waterways to pay respects to the water goddess and symbolize the release of negative energy.

Songkran
Songkran is the Thai New Year celebrated with water fights and cleansing rituals. Participate by engaging in water battles and splashing water on others as a way to start anew.

Thai Cuisine and Dining Etiquette

Sharing is Caring
Thai meals are often communal affairs where dishes are shared among the group. It's customary to take a small portion of each dish rather than piling your plate high.

Chopsticks and Utensils
Use chopsticks for noodle dishes and utensils for other meals. When not using your utensils, rest them on your plate rather than placing them upright in your bowl.

Tasting and Praise

It's polite to taste a bit of every dish to show appreciation for the cook's efforts. If you enjoy a dish, express your enjoyment with a compliment.

Spirit Houses and Superstitions

Spirit Houses

Spirit houses are miniature structures found outside homes and businesses to provide shelter for protective spirits. Show respect by not touching or moving them.

Superstitions

Be mindful of local superstitions, such as not pointing your feet at people, not stepping over food, and avoiding negative language.

Royal Respect

Thai people hold their monarchy in high regard. Treat images of the royal family with respect and avoid any negative discussions about them.

Immersing yourself in Thai traditions and customs is a rewarding way to connect with the heart of the country's culture. By understanding and respecting these practices, you'll not only gain a deeper appreciation for Thailand's heritage but also foster meaningful connections with its people. Whether participating in festivals, visiting temples, or savoring local cuisine, embracing these traditions will enrich your travel experience and leave you with lasting memories of the vibrant and gracious Land of Smiles.

3.2. Discovering Festivals and Celebrations

Thailand is a country that thrives on its vibrant and diverse cultural festivals, making it an ideal destination for families and couples seeking immersive and unique experiences. Throughout the year, the Thai people celebrate a variety of festivals that are deeply rooted in their traditions, beliefs, and history. Participating in these festivals allows travelers to connect with the local culture on a profound level. As you plan your trip to Thailand, understanding and embracing these festivities will undoubtedly enhance your travel experience.

Songkran Festival: Celebrating the Thai New Year

One of the most famous festivals in Thailand, Songkran marks the traditional Thai New Year, usually held from April 13th to 15th. It's renowned for its water fights, where locals and visitors alike engage in friendly water battles to symbolize washing away the old year's troubles and starting anew. Major cities like Bangkok, Chiang Mai, and Phuket turn into joyful water battlegrounds, creating a sense of unity and fun.

Loy Krathong: Festival of Lights

Held on the full moon night of the twelfth lunar month (usually November), Loy Krathong is a mesmerizing festival where people release floating baskets made of banana leaves and decorated with flowers, candles, and incense onto rivers, lakes, and ponds. This act symbolizes letting go of negative energies and making wishes for the future. The sight of thousands of illuminated krathongs floating on the water is a sight to behold.

Yi Peng Lantern Festival

Associated with Loy Krathong, the Yi Peng Lantern Festival in Chiang Mai offers a breathtaking spectacle as thousands of lanterns are released into the night sky, creating a sea of floating lights. The lanterns are believed to carry away bad luck and bring good fortune. Couples can partake in this enchanting event and release lanterns together, making wishes for their future.

Phi Ta Khon: Ghost Festival

Unique to the northeastern province of Loei, the Phi Ta Khon Festival showcases colorful masks, elaborate costumes, and lively parades. Held during June or July, this festival combines fun and spooky elements, as it's believed to wake up the spirits of the deceased. Families can join in the festivities by wearing costumes and masks, dancing to traditional music, and enjoying the vibrant atmosphere.

Vegetarian Festival: Purification and Spiritual Cleansing

Taking place in various Thai-Chinese communities across the country, the Vegetarian Festival occurs during the ninth lunar month (typically September or October). Participants observe a strict vegetarian diet, dress in white, and engage in acts of self-purification to invite good luck and health. Processions featuring impressive displays of body piercing and elaborate rituals are a significant part of this unique event.

King's Birthday and National Father's Day

Celebrated on December 5th, King Bhumibol Adulyadej's birthday is a time of deep respect and reverence for the Thai royal family. This day also coincides with National Father's Day. The city of Bangkok is adorned with lights, decorations, and portraits of the king. Couples and families can join in the celebrations by visiting the Grand Palace and observing the ceremonies held in honor of the king.

Long Boat Races: Teamwork and Excitement
Long boat races are held in various locations across Thailand, typically from August to November. These races are a thrilling spectacle of teamwork and athleticism as teams of rowers compete in long, colorful boats. The most famous event takes place in Phichit, where visitors can witness the exhilarating races and experience the festive atmosphere.

Thai Boxing Festivals: Muay Thai Culture
For those interested in sports and martial arts, attending a Muay Thai boxing match is a must. While not a traditional festival in the same sense as others, Muay Thai fights are a cultural experience that provides insight into Thai traditions and athleticism. Major stadiums in Bangkok, such as Lumpinee Boxing Stadium and Rajadamnern Stadium, host regular matches.

Makha Bucha: Spiritual Reflection
Makha Bucha falls on the full moon day of the third lunar month (usually February). This Buddhist holiday commemorates the day when 1,250 monks

spontaneously gathered to hear a sermon from Buddha. Locals and visitors alike participate in candlelight processions around temples, engaging in meditative practices and reflecting on the teachings of Buddhism.

Chiang Mai Flower Festival: Blossoms and Beauty

Held during the first weekend of February, the Chiang Mai Flower Festival showcases the region's stunning flora. The event features vibrant parades of flower-decorated floats, traditional dances, and exhibitions of elaborate flower arrangements. Couples can stroll through the flower-filled streets, taking in the colorful beauty of the city.

As you plan your journey to Thailand, consider the timing of these festivals and how they align with your travel dates. Participating in these celebrations will not only provide you with unforgettable memories but also deepen your understanding of Thai culture and traditions. Remember to respect local customs and engage with the festivities in a mindful and appreciative manner.

3.3. Trying Out Traditional Thai Cuisine

One of the most exciting aspects of traveling to Thailand is undoubtedly the opportunity to indulge in its rich and diverse culinary scene. Thai cuisine is celebrated for its harmonious blend of flavors, textures, and aromas, often striking a balance between sweet, sour, salty, and spicy elements. Exploring traditional Thai cuisine is not only a delightful gastronomic experience but also a window into the country's culture and history. From street food stalls to upscale restaurants, Thailand offers a plethora of options for families and couples to savor authentic dishes that cater to a wide range of tastes.

Rice: The Heart of Thai Cuisine

Rice is a staple in Thai cuisine and forms the foundation of most meals. Jasmine rice, known for its fragrant aroma and soft texture, is often served alongside a variety of dishes. Families and couples can enjoy rice in various forms, from steamed white rice to flavorful fried rice dishes.

Thai Street Food: A Flavorful Adventure

Thailand's street food scene is legendary, offering an array of mouthwatering options that showcase the country's culinary creativity. Families can sample dishes like pad Thai (stir-fried noodles), som tam (spicy green papaya salad), and moo ping (grilled pork skewers). Couples can bond over exploring bustling night markets and sharing small bites from different vendors.

Tom Yum Goong: The Quintessential Thai Soup

Tom Yum Goong is a bold and fragrant hot and sour soup that exemplifies the complexity of Thai flavors. Made with shrimp, mushrooms, lemongrass, kaffir lime leaves, and chili peppers, this soup offers a delightful interplay between tangy and spicy notes. Families and couples can relish the aromatic experience of Tom Yum Goong together.

Green Curry: A Creamy and Spicy Delight

Thai curries are a culinary masterpiece, and the green curry is a popular favorite. Made with a blend of green chilies, coconut milk, and fresh herbs, this dish is known for its vibrant color and aromatic richness. Families and couples can enjoy green curry with chicken, beef, or tofu, accompanied by steamed rice.

Pad Thai: A Taste of Thailand's Streets

Pad Thai is perhaps one of the most iconic Thai dishes known worldwide. Stir-fried rice noodles are combined with eggs, tamarind sauce, shrimp or chicken, and various toppings like peanuts and bean sprouts. Families and couples can savor this flavorful creation, often customized to suit individual preferences.

Massaman Curry: A Fusion of Flavors

Massaman curry is a testament to Thailand's historical connections with India and the Middle East. This rich and nutty curry features tender chunks of meat (usually beef) simmered in coconut milk and spiced with a blend of cardamom, cinnamon, and nutmeg. Its unique taste offers a culinary journey for both families and couples.

Som Tam: Spicy and Refreshing

Som Tam, or green papaya salad, is a zesty dish that perfectly balances spicy, sour, and sweet flavors. Families and couples can relish the crunchy texture of shredded green papaya, paired with ingredients like tomatoes, lime, fish sauce, and chili peppers. This dish is both refreshing and invigorating.

Mango Sticky Rice: A Sweet Finale

No exploration of Thai cuisine is complete without indulging in the beloved dessert, mango sticky rice. Families and couples can end their meals on a sweet note with this combination of ripe mango slices and glutinous rice drizzled with sweet coconut milk. The contrast between the tender rice and the juicy mango creates a delectable symphony of flavors.

Culinary Workshops: Immersion in Thai Cooking

For families and couples seeking a deeper connection to Thai cuisine, participating in a cooking workshop is a fantastic idea. Many places across Thailand offer hands-on classes that guide participants through the preparation of traditional dishes. This not only provides a memorable experience but also equips travelers with skills to recreate Thai dishes at home.

Dining Etiquette: Embracing Thai Culture

When enjoying traditional Thai cuisine, it's important to respect local dining customs. Families and couples can immerse themselves in Thai culture by practicing etiquette such as sharing dishes, using utensils mindfully, and paying respects before meals.

Exploring traditional Thai cuisine is an adventure in itself, allowing families and couples to bond over shared meals, discover new flavors, and connect with the local way of life. Whether indulging in street food or dining in upscale establishments, the culinary journey through Thailand promises an unforgettable experience that will leave a lasting impression on your travel memories.

CHAPTER 4: Top Family-Friendly Destinations

4.1. Bangkok: Urban Excitement for All Ages

Bangkok, the vibrant capital of Thailand, is a city that seamlessly blends tradition with modernity, creating an urban playground that appeals to travelers of all ages. From bustling markets and historical temples to cutting-edge shopping malls and lively nightlife, Bangkok offers a kaleidoscope of experiences that families and couples can enjoy together. This chapter will guide you through the many facets of Bangkok, ensuring that your visit to this dynamic city is both memorable and rewarding.

Grand Palace and Wat Phra Kaew: A Glimpse into Thailand's Heritage

Begin your exploration of Bangkok by immersing yourself in its rich history and culture at the Grand Palace and Wat Phra Kaew, the Temple of the Emerald Buddha. The opulent architecture, intricate details, and spiritual significance of these landmarks offer an enlightening experience for both families and couples. Witness the awe-inspiring beauty of the Emerald Buddha, a revered image that is meticulously adorned in different seasonal outfits.

Wat Arun: The Temple of Dawn
Located along the Chao Phraya River, Wat Arun
stands as a stunning architectural marvel. Families
and couples can ascend the temple's central prang
to take in panoramic views of the city, particularly
at sunrise or sunset when the temple's spires are
bathed in golden light. The intricate ceramic mosaic
work on the temple's façade is a testament to
Thailand's artistic craftsmanship.

**Chao Phraya River: A Journey Through
Bangkok's Heart**
Embark on a Chao Phraya River cruise to gain a
unique perspective of Bangkok's urban landscape.
Families can enjoy the scenic views while couples
can relish the romantic ambiance. Along the
riverbanks, you'll encounter cultural landmarks,
bustling markets, and picturesque temples that
provide a glimpse into the city's daily life.

**Chatuchak Weekend Market: Shopping
Extravaganza**
For families and couples who love shopping and
exploring vibrant markets, the Chatuchak Weekend
Market is a must-visit destination. With thousands
of stalls selling everything from clothing and
accessories to handicrafts and antiques, this

sprawling market promises an exciting and eclectic shopping experience.

Bangkok's Street Food: A Culinary Adventure

The bustling streets of Bangkok are a food lover's paradise. Families and couples can indulge in a diverse array of street food offerings, from savory pad Thai and crispy fried chicken to exotic fruits and delectable desserts. Dining at street food stalls not only offers an authentic taste of Thai cuisine but also immerses you in the lively street culture of the city.

Siam Square: Shopping and Entertainment Hub

Siam Square is a modern district that pulsates with energy. Families can explore mega-malls like Siam Paragon, where attractions like SEA LIFE Bangkok Ocean World offer an underwater adventure. Couples can relish high-end shopping, catch a movie, or simply stroll through the vibrant streets adorned with innovative street art.

Jim Thompson House: A Slice of Thai Heritage

The Jim Thompson House is a hidden gem that provides insight into the life of the American silk entrepreneur who played a pivotal role in reviving Thailand's silk industry. Families and couples can explore the beautifully preserved traditional Thai house, surrounded by lush gardens and exquisite art collections.

Asiatique the Riverfront: Night Bazaar and Entertainment

Asiatique offers a fusion of shopping, dining, and entertainment along the Chao Phraya River. Families can enjoy a Ferris wheel ride, browse through boutiques, and savor international and Thai cuisine. For couples seeking a romantic evening, the riverfront setting, illuminated by lights and adorned with colorful decorations, creates an enchanting ambiance.

Lumphini Park: Urban Oasis

Amidst the urban chaos of Bangkok, Lumphini Park serves as a tranquil oasis where families and couples can escape the city's hustle and bustle. Enjoy a leisurely stroll, rent a paddleboat on the lake, or join a free aerobics session in the evening. The park's lush greenery and serene atmosphere provide a welcome respite.

Bangkok's Nightlife: Lively Entertainment

As the sun sets, Bangkok's nightlife comes alive with a myriad of options. While families may choose to attend traditional Thai puppet shows or cultural performances, couples can explore the city's trendy rooftop bars, live music venues, and nightclubs that offer an energetic and unforgettable night out.

Bangkok's dynamic blend of tradition and modernity creates a city that captivates travelers of all ages. Families and couples can explore its historic landmarks, savor its vibrant street food culture, shop in diverse markets, and immerse themselves in its artistic and culinary offerings. From dawn to dusk, Bangkok promises an urban adventure that leaves a lasting impression on every visitor's heart. Whether you're seeking cultural enrichment or exhilarating experiences, Bangkok's urban excitement has something to offer everyone, making it a perfect destination for families and couples alike.

4.2. Chiang Mai: Nature and Culture Delights

Nestled in the lush mountains of northern Thailand, Chiang Mai is a city that beckons travelers with its harmonious blend of natural beauty and rich cultural heritage. Known for its serene landscapes, intricate temples, and vibrant arts scene, Chiang Mai offers families and couples an enchanting escape from the bustle of urban life. This chapter will guide you through the captivating nature and cultural treasures that await you in this charming city.

Doi Suthep Temple: A Spiritual Journey

Start your exploration of Chiang Mai with a visit to Wat Phra That Doi Suthep, a temple perched atop Doi Suthep mountain. Families and couples can climb the 306 steps adorned with mythical serpents to reach the temple, where a revered golden chedi and panoramic views of the city await. Witness the devotion of locals as they offer prayers and make merit.

Chiang Mai Old City: Stepping into the Past

The heart of Chiang Mai lies within its ancient walls, where families and couples can immerse themselves in the city's history and culture. Explore the narrow alleyways, visit historic temples like Wat Chedi Luang, and engage with local artisans in the bustling markets. The old city's charm and authenticity offer a glimpse into Chiang Mai's storied past.

Elephant Sanctuaries: Ethical Encounters

Chiang Mai is renowned for its elephant sanctuaries that prioritize the well-being and conservation of these magnificent creatures. Families and couples can experience the joy of interacting with elephants in a responsible and ethical manner, participating in activities such as feeding, bathing, and observing their natural behavior. Examples include Elephant Nature Park and Patara Elephant Farm.

Night Bazaar: Shopping and Cultural Exploration

Chiang Mai's Night Bazaar is a lively hub where families and couples can browse through a variety of handicrafts, textiles, and artworks. Enjoy the vibrant atmosphere as street performers entertain and vendors offer a delightful array of local products. This is an ideal place to purchase souvenirs that reflect Chiang Mai's artistic heritage.

Chiang Mai Flower Festival: A Burst of Color

If you're visiting in February, the Chiang Mai Flower Festival is a visual feast that showcases the region's vibrant flora. Families and couples can witness colorful parades featuring intricately designed floats adorned with flowers. This event provides a perfect opportunity to enjoy the beauty of nature while celebrating Chiang Mai's cultural traditions.

Doi Inthanon National Park: Nature's Majesty

Venture to Doi Inthanon, Thailand's highest peak, to explore a haven of natural beauty. Families and couples can hike through lush forests, discover stunning waterfalls, and breathe in the crisp mountain air. The Twin Royal Pagodas at the summit offer breathtaking views and a tranquil space for reflection.

Thai Cooking Classes: A Culinary Adventure

Immerse yourself in the flavors of Chiang Mai by participating in a Thai cooking class. Families and couples can learn to prepare traditional dishes using fresh ingredients and age-old techniques. The experience provides insights into Thai culture and equips you with culinary skills to recreate authentic dishes at home.

Art and Craft Studios: Creative Exploration

Chiang Mai's artistic community thrives in its many studios and workshops. Families can engage in hands-on experiences like pottery-making or traditional weaving. Couples can appreciate the intricate details of local craftsmanship, from intricate wood carvings to delicate silk textiles.

Loy Krathong and Yi Peng Festivals: Illuminating the Night

If your visit aligns with November's full moon, you'll have the chance to witness the Loy Krathong and Yi Peng festivals. Families and couples release lanterns into the night sky and float krathongs (decorated baskets) on water bodies, symbolizing the release of negativity and making wishes for the future.

Hill Tribe Villages: Cultural Encounters

Venture beyond Chiang Mai to experience the unique cultures of the hill tribe communities. Families and couples can visit villages like the Karen or Hmong, interacting with locals, learning about their traditions, and appreciating their intricate crafts. Be sure to approach these encounters with respect and cultural sensitivity.

Chiang Mai's allure lies in its ability to offer both nature and cultural experiences that cater to families and couples seeking an enriching journey. From exploring ancient temples and vibrant markets to immersing oneself in the tranquility of natural landscapes and ethical wildlife encounters,

Chiang Mai provides a diverse array of experiences that resonate with travelers of all ages. Its blend of tradition and natural beauty makes Chiang Mai an unforgettable destination that promises to captivate your senses and leave a lasting impression. Whether you're seeking spiritual enlightenment, artistic exploration, or a tranquil escape, Chiang Mai's nature and culture delights are sure to enchant and inspire.

4.3. Phuket: Beach Bliss and Water Adventures

Phuket, Thailand's largest island, is a tropical paradise that beckons families and couples with its pristine beaches, crystal-clear waters, and a plethora of water-based activities. From thrilling water adventures to serene beach getaways, Phuket offers an idyllic destination where nature and adventure seamlessly merge. This chapter will guide you through the beach bliss and exhilarating water experiences that await you in this coastal haven.

Patong Beach: The Heart of Phuket's Action

Kickstart your Phuket adventure with a visit to Patong Beach, the island's most famous and bustling beach destination. Families and couples can enjoy a vibrant atmosphere, indulge in watersports, and explore the lively Patong Beach Road lined with restaurants, shops, and entertainment venues. As the sun sets, Patong transforms into a hub of nightlife, offering entertainment options for all ages.

Phi Phi Islands: Tropical Paradise Awaits
Embark on a boat trip to the Phi Phi Islands, an archipelago known for its stunning beauty and vibrant marine life. Families can explore snorkeling spots teeming with colorful fish, while couples can bask in the romantic ambiance of secluded coves and breathtaking viewpoints. Maya Bay, made famous by the movie "The Beach," is a must-visit destination.

Similan Islands: Diving and Snorkeling Haven
For families and couples seeking an underwater adventure, the Similan Islands National Park is a haven for divers and snorkelers. The park boasts vibrant coral reefs, diverse marine species, and clear waters. Whether you're an experienced diver or a novice snorkeler, the Similan Islands offer an opportunity to explore the wonders of the Andaman Sea.

Phang Nga Bay: Majestic Limestone Karsts
Phang Nga Bay's dramatic limestone karsts rising
from emerald waters create a surreal landscape that
families and couples can explore through boat
tours. The bay's unique topography includes hidden
caves, tranquil lagoons, and the iconic James Bond
Island. Kayaking through the bay's serene waters is
a memorable way to appreciate its natural beauty
up close.

Kata and Karon Beaches: Tranquil Retreats
Escape the crowds and indulge in a serene beach
experience at Kata and Karon Beaches. Families
and couples can relax on the soft sands, swim in
calm waters, and enjoy the slower pace of these
quieter beaches. The sunset views from Kata
Viewpoint are particularly captivating and offer a
romantic backdrop for couples.

Phuket FantaSea: Cultural Extravaganza
Phuket FantaSea is a theme park that offers a
cultural spectacle combining traditional Thai
elements with modern entertainment. Families and
couples can enjoy a vibrant buffet dinner, dazzling
stage performances, and a carnival-like
atmosphere. The show's fusion of magic, acrobatics,
and storytelling creates an enchanting experience
for all ages.

James Bond Island: Iconic Landmark

Made famous by the James Bond film "The Man with the Golden Gun," this unique island is characterized by its solitary limestone pinnacle jutting out of the sea. Families and couples can explore the island's stunning natural beauty by boat, kayak, or guided tour, appreciating its cinematic allure and photogenic landscapes.

Snuba Diving: A Blend of Snorkeling and Scuba Diving

Ideal for families and couples seeking a middle ground between snorkeling and scuba diving, snuba diving allows you to explore the underwater world without the need for extensive training. Snuba combines the simplicity of snorkeling with the ability to dive deeper and experience marine life up close.

Old Phuket Town: A Glimpse into the Past

Immerse yourself in Phuket's cultural heritage by exploring Old Phuket Town. Families and couples can wander through colorful streets adorned with Sino-Portuguese architecture, boutique shops, and street art. The town's vibrant history and charming ambiance make it an ideal place for cultural exploration and leisurely strolls.

Sunset Cruises: Romantic Sailings

End your days in Phuket with a romantic sunset cruise. Families and couples can embark on a relaxing boat journey as the sun dips below the horizon, painting the sky with a spectrum of colors. Many cruises offer onboard dining and entertainment, creating a memorable and romantic experience.

Phuket's allure lies in its ability to cater to families and couples seeking a harmonious blend of beach relaxation and aquatic adventures. From its sun-kissed beaches and turquoise waters to its vibrant marine life and cultural attractions, Phuket offers a diverse range of experiences that resonate with travelers of all ages. Its tropical beauty and exhilarating water activities make Phuket an enticing destination that promises to captivate your senses and create lasting memories. Whether you're seeking adrenaline-pumping water sports or tranquil beachfront moments, Phuket's beach bliss and water adventures are sure to enchant and invigorate your spirit.

CHAPTER 5: Romantic Getaways

5.1. A Stroll Through the Enchanting Streets of Chiang Rai

Nestled in the northernmost region of Thailand, Chiang Rai stands as a hidden gem that beckons travelers with its mesmerizing blend of natural beauty, cultural heritage, and warm hospitality. As you embark on a journey through this enchanting city, you will find yourself captivated by its vibrant streets, ancient temples, bustling markets, and serene landscapes. In this chapter of our travel guidebook, we invite you to join us on a virtual stroll through the alluring streets of Chiang Rai, where tradition meets modernity in the most captivating manner.

A Glimpse into Chiang Rai's Rich Heritage:

Chiang Rai's history dates back to the 13th century when it was established as the capital of the Lanna Kingdom. This legacy is beautifully preserved in the city's architecture, customs, and traditions. Your stroll through Chiang Rai's streets will reveal a tapestry of influences from neighboring countries, leaving you with a sense of awe and wonder at the city's cultural depth.

The Radiance of Wat Rong Khun (White Temple):

Our journey begins with a visit to one of Chiang Rai's most iconic landmarks, the ethereal Wat Rong Khun, commonly known as the White Temple. This contemporary masterpiece is a fusion of traditional Thai architecture and modern artistic expression. As you approach, the gleaming white facade adorned with intricate mirror mosaics will leave you spellbound. The temple's symbolism is equally profound, reflecting the contrast between good and evil through its design elements. Don't miss the chance to marvel at the breathtaking murals that grace the interior walls, a stunning reinterpretation of traditional Buddhist art with pop culture references.

Immerse Yourself in Hill Tribe Culture:

Chiang Rai is a cultural melting pot, home to several indigenous hill tribes, each with their unique customs and way of life. A stroll through the city's streets will lead you to vibrant markets where you can engage with members of these tribes, such as the Akha, Karen, and Hmong. These encounters offer a glimpse into their distinctive attire, intricate handicrafts, and traditional practices, fostering a deeper understanding of Thailand's diverse cultural landscape.

Chiang Rai's Night Bazaar:

As the sun sets, the city's energy takes on a new rhythm, and the Chiang Rai Night Bazaar comes alive. Here, you can lose yourself in a maze of stalls offering an array of goods, from handmade textiles and jewelry to local street food delicacies. Engage in the art of bargaining as you explore the bustling market, and be sure to try Khao Soi, a northern Thai noodle curry dish that embodies the region's flavors.

Phra Kaew Temple and the City's Spiritual Heart:

Our journey continues to Phra Kaew Temple, where Chiang Rai's spiritual heart beats. The temple houses the sacred Emerald Buddha, which once resided in Chiang Rai before finding its place in Bangkok's Grand Palace. This temple complex showcases intricate wood carvings and stunning Lanna architecture, creating an atmosphere of reverence and tranquility. Explore the surrounding gardens, and perhaps even engage in a moment of meditation as you soak in the serene surroundings.

Discover the Intrigue of the Golden Clock Tower:

Chiang Rai's Golden Clock Tower stands as a beacon of modern design amidst its historical backdrop. Lit up in the evening, the tower exudes an otherworldly glow that reflects off its golden surface. Be sure to time your visit for when the tower's lights and music show take place, transforming the area into a magical spectacle that is sure to delight both the young and the young at heart.

Riverside Serenity at Kok River:

Escape the bustle of the city streets and head towards the tranquil banks of the Kok River. A leisurely stroll along the riverside will introduce you to scenes of traditional Thai life. Watch as locals engage in fishing or navigate the river on traditional wooden boats. You might consider embarking on a relaxing boat ride, allowing you to fully immerse yourself in the region's picturesque landscapes.

Mae Fah Luang Art and Cultural Park:

Concluding our stroll, we invite you to explore the Mae Fah Luang Art and Cultural Park, a space that celebrates the rich artistic heritage of the Lanna Kingdom. The park features an extensive collection of artifacts, including sculptures, paintings, and traditional textiles. Stroll through the beautifully landscaped gardens, and appreciate the harmonious fusion of art and nature.

Chiang Rai's enchanting streets weave a tale of tradition and modernity, inviting travelers to embark on a journey that transcends time. From the awe-inspiring White Temple to the serenity of the Kok River, the city captivates with its unique blend of historical depth and contemporary vibrancy. A stroll through Chiang Rai's enchanting streets offers a glimpse into the soul of northern Thailand, leaving an indelible mark on the hearts of all who venture there. So, pack your curiosity, and let Chiang Rai's captivating charm unfold with each step you take.

5.2. Island Retreats: Koh Samui and Krabi

Imagine a place where azure waters kiss powder-soft beaches, where lush tropical landscapes embrace dramatic limestone cliffs, and where relaxation takes on a whole new meaning. Welcome to the paradise islands of Koh Samui and Krabi in Thailand. In this chapter of our travel guidebook, we invite you to embark on an unforgettable journey of rejuvenation, exploration, and enchantment as we delve into the allure of Koh Samui's serenity and Krabi's natural splendor.

Koh Samui: Serenity and Blissful Escapes:

Chaweng Beach: A Vibrant Playground by the Sea:

Our journey begins on the shores of Koh Samui, where Chaweng Beach reigns as a hub of activity and leisure. This expansive stretch of golden sand is flanked by a variety of resorts, restaurants, and shops, catering to all kinds of travelers. Lounge under the swaying palm trees, dip your toes in the crystal-clear waters, or explore the local markets for a taste of Koh Samui's vibrant culture.

Big Buddha Temple: A Symbol of Spiritual Grandeur:

A visit to Koh Samui is incomplete without paying homage to the island's revered landmark, the Big

Buddha Temple (Wat Phra Yai). Set atop a hill, the monumental golden statue of the Buddha overlooks the island, exuding an air of serenity and spirituality. The temple complex features ornate architecture, intricate shrines, and breathtaking views of the coastline below.

Ang Thong Marine Park: A Nature Lover's Haven:

For those seeking an adventure beyond the shores, a trip to Ang Thong Marine Park is a must. A collection of pristine islands and turquoise waters, this marine park offers opportunities for snorkeling, kayaking, and hiking amidst untouched nature. Explore hidden lagoons, marvel at unique rock formations, and bask in the untouched beauty of this natural wonderland.

Fisherman's Village: A Glimpse of Island Heritage:

Retreat to the quaint charm of Fisherman's Village in Bophut, where the island's history and culture come to life. Cobblestone streets are lined with old wooden houses, boutique shops, and a lively Friday Night Market. Sample local delicacies, shop for handmade crafts, and savor the island's fusion of tradition and modernity.

Krabi: Nature's Canvas of Limestone Wonders:

Railay Beach: A Hidden Gem Accessible by Boat:

Our journey continues to Krabi, where Railay Beach stands as an epitome of untouched beauty. Accessible only by boat due to its dramatic limestone cliffs, Railay offers a secluded paradise for beach lovers and rock climbers alike. Explore the hidden lagoons, indulge in rock climbing adventures, or simply bask in the tranquility of this natural haven.

Ao Nang: The Gateway to Krabi's Treasures:

As the main tourist hub of Krabi, Ao Nang serves as the perfect base for island hopping and exploring the nearby attractions. With a vibrant nightlife, an array of dining options, and stunning sunset views, Ao Nang adds a touch of modern comfort to your island retreat.

Phi Phi Islands: An Archipelago of Wonders:

A short boat ride from Krabi, the Phi Phi Islands offer a postcard-perfect escape into turquoise waters, dramatic cliffs, and vibrant marine life. Maya Bay, made famous by the film "The Beach," is just one of the many breathtaking spots that await exploration. Snorkel, swim, or simply lounge on the white sand beaches as you soak in the natural beauty.

Thung Teao Forest Natural Park: The Enchanting Emerald Pool:

Nestled within the lush greenery of Krabi, the Thung Teao Forest Natural Park houses the stunning Emerald Pool. True to its name, the pool's crystal-clear waters take on an enchanting emerald hue. A short hike through the jungle brings you to this natural wonder, providing a refreshing and rejuvenating experience amidst nature.

As our exploration of Koh Samui's serenity and Krabi's natural beauty comes to a close, we're left with memories of breathtaking landscapes, tranquil beaches, and captivating cultural encounters. Whether you seek moments of relaxation by the sea or adventures in unspoiled nature, these island retreats offer a harmonious blend of tranquility and exploration. Koh Samui and Krabi, with their unique charms, are a testament to the diversity and enchantment that Thailand's islands have to offer. So pack your bags, bring your sense of wonder, and prepare to be swept away by the allure of these two captivating paradises.

5.3. Tranquil Escapes to Pai and Hua Hin

Nestled in the heart of Thailand, away from the bustling cities and tourist crowds, lie two hidden gems that promise an escape into tranquility and natural beauty. In this chapter of our travel guidebook, we invite you to journey with us to the serene havens of Pai and Hua Hin. These destinations offer a peaceful retreat from the ordinary, where the pace of life slows down, and travelers can immerse themselves in the harmonious blend of nature, culture, and relaxation.

Pai: Embracing Nature's Embrace and Cultural Charms:

Pai Canyon: Walking on the Edge of Adventure:

Our journey begins in Pai, a picturesque town known for its lush landscapes and vibrant arts scene. The Pai Canyon, a natural wonder of eroded red sandstone, is a must-visit destination. As you navigate the narrow paths that wind along the edge of the cliffs, you're rewarded with breathtaking panoramic views of the surrounding valleys and mountains. Sunset here is a sight to behold, casting a golden glow over the rugged terrain.

Pam Bok Waterfall: Refreshing Oasis of Serenity:

Escape the heat and immerse yourself in the refreshing waters of Pam Bok Waterfall. A short hike through the jungle reveals this hidden gem, where cascading water creates a soothing melody amidst the verdant foliage. Take a dip in the natural pool, surrounded by the calming embrace of nature, and let your worries wash away.

Tha Pai Hot Springs: Soothing Relaxation in Nature's Jacuzzi:

Indulge in the ultimate relaxation at Tha Pai Hot Springs, where natural mineral-rich waters bubble up from the earth. These therapeutic hot springs are believed to offer a range of health benefits. Nestled within a tranquil garden, you can choose between soaking in the individual hot tubs or dipping your feet into the streams, all while surrounded by the beauty of the forest.

Walking Street and Pai Night Market: Local Delights and Handicrafts:

As evening falls, the town comes alive with the vibrant atmosphere of Walking Street and Pai Night Market. Meander through stalls offering a diverse range of local snacks, handmade crafts, and clothing. This is the perfect opportunity to interact with local artisans, sample traditional delicacies, and perhaps find a unique souvenir to remember your time in Pai.

Hua Hin: Coastal Elegance and Leisurely Retreats:

Hua Hin Beach: Tranquility by the Sea:

Our journey continues to Hua Hin, a charming coastal town renowned for its royal heritage and relaxed ambiance. Hua Hin Beach stretches along the Gulf of Thailand, inviting visitors to stroll along its soft sands, take a leisurely swim, or simply bask in the soothing sounds of the waves. The sunrise and sunset views from the beach are particularly enchanting.

Hua Hin Railway Station: Nostalgic Beauty and Royal Connections:

A visit to the Hua Hin Railway Station is like stepping back in time. This historical station, with its ornate architecture and vibrant gardens, offers a glimpse into Thailand's past. Notably, it played a role in Hua Hin's royal legacy, as it was the chosen route for King Rama VI to travel to his summer palace, Klai Kangwon Palace.

Klai Kangwon Palace: Royalty and Elegance by the Sea:

The Klai Kangwon Palace, also known as the "Far From Worries Palace," remains the official residence of the Thai royal family. While the palace itself is not open to the public, the surrounding gardens are accessible. Stroll through the manicured lawns, fragrant flower beds, and take in the tranquil views of the sea, imagining the serene retreat that the palace offers to the royal family.

Cicada Market: Artistic Expression and Culinary Delights:

Immerse yourself in Hua Hin's creative spirit at the Cicada Market, a vibrant night market that celebrates local art, music, and culinary excellence. This market is a haven for art enthusiasts, with galleries, live performances, and craft stalls showcasing the talents of local artists. Indulge in a variety of Thai and international dishes, all while enjoying the lively atmosphere.

As we conclude our exploration of Pai and Hua Hin, it's evident that both destinations offer a respite from the fast-paced world, allowing travelers to rediscover the beauty of simplicity and serenity. Whether you're seeking the artistic charm of Pai or the coastal elegance of Hua Hin, these tranquil escapes promise a harmonious blend of nature, culture, and relaxation. From the rugged landscapes of Pai to the coastal allure of Hua Hin, both destinations invite you to unwind, recharge, and immerse yourself in the unique charm that only Thailand can offer. So pack your bags, leave your worries behind, and embark on a journey to discover the hidden tranquility of Pai and the timeless allure of Hua Hin.

CHAPTER 6: Activities for Kids and Couples

6.1. Elephants and Nature: Ethical Wildlife Experiences

When it comes to experiencing the majesty of Thailand's wildlife, there's nothing quite like encountering the gentle giants of the animal kingdom: elephants. As stewards of the land, these magnificent creatures are deeply intertwined with the country's culture and history. In this chapter of our travel guidebook, we will delve into the world of ethical elephant encounters and nature-focused experiences in Thailand. By prioritizing the well-being of these incredible animals and respecting the environment, you can create memories that will last a lifetime while contributing to conservation efforts.

The Importance of Ethical Wildlife Encounters:

Before embarking on any wildlife adventure, it's crucial to understand the significance of ethical experiences. Over the years, the tourism industry has exploited animals for profit, leading to distressing conditions for animals and ecological imbalance. Ethical wildlife encounters prioritize the welfare of animals, conservation efforts, and responsible tourism practices. When choosing experiences, look for sanctuaries and programs that prioritize the well-being of animals, promote education, and actively contribute to environmental conservation.

Elephant Sanctuaries: Respecting and Protecting these Majestic Creatures:

Elephant Nature Park, Chiang Mai: A Haven of Compassion:

One of Thailand's most well-known and respected elephant sanctuaries is the Elephant Nature Park in Chiang Mai. This sanctuary provides a safe haven for rescued elephants, allowing them to live freely in their natural habitat. Visitors have the opportunity to observe these animals in their element, feed them, and even bathe them in the river—all while learning about the challenges elephants face and the importance of conservation efforts.

Boon Lott's Elephant Sanctuary, Sukhothai: Creating Lasting Bonds:

Boon Lott's Elephant Sanctuary in Sukhothai focuses on creating meaningful connections between humans and elephants. This sanctuary places an emphasis on letting elephants roam freely, form their own social groups, and interact with visitors on their terms. Engage in hands-off activities that prioritize the well-being of the elephants, and gain insights into their behavior and natural environment.

Nature-Centric Experiences: Preserving Thailand's Biodiversity:

Khao Sok National Park: Exploring the Oldest Rainforest:

For nature enthusiasts, Khao Sok National Park is a must-visit destination. This ancient rainforest boasts diverse flora and fauna, including rare species of birds, reptiles, and mammals. Embark on guided treks, canoe rides through pristine rivers, and stay in eco-friendly accommodations to immerse yourself in the untouched beauty of Thailand's wilderness.

Doi Inthanon National Park: The Roof of Thailand:

Venture to Doi Inthanon, the highest peak in Thailand, located in Chiang Mai. This national park features lush forests, waterfalls, and a wide array of bird species. Explore the hiking trails, visit the Royal Pagodas, and revel in the breathtaking vistas that extend over the mist-covered mountains.

Ao Phang Nga National Park: A Paradise of Limestone Karsts:

Experience the unique landscapes of Ao Phang Nga National Park, known for its iconic limestone karsts and emerald waters. Take a boat tour through the mangrove forests, kayak in hidden lagoons, and visit James Bond Island, made famous by the film "The Man with the Golden Gun."

Sustainable Travel Practices: Nurturing a Brighter Future:

Choose Certified and Accredited Experiences:

Opt for experiences that have been accredited by recognized organizations, such as the Global Sustainable Tourism Council (GSTC), which ensures that ethical and sustainable practices are upheld.

Support Local Communities:

Participate in activities that benefit local communities and promote their involvement in conservation efforts. These interactions contribute to the preservation of cultural heritage and local economies.

Responsible Photography:

When interacting with wildlife, prioritize their comfort and well-being over capturing the perfect shot. Avoid close contact or flash photography that may disturb the animals.

Leave No Trace:

Respect the environment by following the principles of "Leave No Trace." Carry out all waste, avoid damaging flora and fauna, and minimize your impact on the natural surroundings.

Thailand's ethically focused wildlife encounters and nature-centric experiences allow you to forge a deeper connection with the country's diverse ecosystems and remarkable creatures. By prioritizing the well-being of animals and the preservation of nature, you can play a crucial role in promoting sustainable tourism and conservation efforts. Whether you choose to interact with elephants in their sanctuaries or explore the pristine landscapes of national parks, your journey will be imbued with a sense of awe, appreciation, and responsibility for the beautiful world that Thailand holds. Embrace these ethical adventures, leaving behind a positive footprint that ensures future generations can enjoy the wonders of Thailand's wildlife and nature.

6.2. Beach Fun: Sandcastles, Snorkeling, and Beyond

With its stunning coastline stretching along the Andaman Sea and the Gulf of Thailand, Thailand is a beach lover's paradise. In this chapter of our travel guidebook, we invite you to indulge in the ultimate beach fun experience in Thailand. From building intricate sandcastles to exploring vibrant underwater worlds through snorkeling, the Thai beaches offer a wealth of activities for every kind of traveler. Join us as we dive into the sun-soaked world of beach adventures, where relaxation and excitement go hand in hand.

The Art of Sandcastles:

Patong Beach, Phuket: Sculpting Dreams in the Sand:

Patong Beach, located in the vibrant city of Phuket, is not only a hotspot for nightlife but also a canvas for creative sandcastle enthusiasts. Here, the powdery sands become your artistic medium as you craft elaborate sand sculptures. Engage with local sand artists who are often more than happy to share their expertise and techniques. Whether you're building a sandcastle masterpiece or admiring the intricate creations of others, Patong Beach offers a playful and artistic escape.

Railay Beach, Krabi: Coastal Canvas of Imagination:

Railay Beach in Krabi is renowned for its stunning limestone cliffs and turquoise waters. This tranquil paradise provides the perfect backdrop for sandcastle enthusiasts. Let your creativity run wild as you sculpt intricate designs, fortresses, and sculptures in the soft sand. The serene atmosphere and breathtaking views add an extra layer of inspiration to your sandy creations.

Snorkeling: Exploring Thailand's Underwater Treasures:

Similan Islands: A Snorkeler's Paradise:

The Similan Islands, situated in the Andaman Sea, are a haven for snorkelers seeking to explore Thailand's underwater beauty. Crystal-clear waters reveal vibrant coral reefs teeming with colorful marine life. Glide alongside graceful sea turtles, schools of tropical fish, and intricate coral formations that create a mesmerizing underwater tapestry.

Koh Tao: Diving into a World of Marine Marvels:

Known as the "Turtle Island," Koh Tao is a haven for snorkelers and divers alike. The island's shallow bays provide excellent opportunities for snorkeling, where you can encounter playful reef fish, graceful rays, and, if you're lucky, majestic whale sharks. Don't miss the chance to explore the vibrant underwater landscapes and witness the intricate dance of life beneath the waves.

Beyond the Beach: Coastal Activities and Adventures:

Paddleboarding: Glide on Tranquil Waters:

Embrace the serene beauty of Thailand's coastlines from a paddleboard. Popular beaches like Kata Beach in Phuket and Ao Nang in Krabi offer paddle board rentals, allowing you to glide over calm waters and enjoy the breathtaking views of the surrounding landscapes.

Sea Kayaking: Exploring Hidden Coves and Caves:

Rent a sea kayak and embark on an exploration of hidden coves, secluded beaches, and mystical sea caves. Koh Hong in Krabi is particularly known for its breathtaking limestone cliffs and emerald waters, making it an ideal destination for sea kayaking adventures.

Sunset Beach Parties: Dance the Night Away:

As the sun dips below the horizon, Thailand's beaches transform into lively party venues. Join fellow travelers at renowned beach bars and clubs, such as the Full Moon Party in Koh Phangan or the beach clubs of Patong Beach in Phuket. Dance to vibrant beats, enjoy fire shows, and revel in the energetic atmosphere that defines Thailand's beach nightlife.

Thailand's beaches offer an endless playground for those seeking sun, sand, and sea. From the artistic pursuits of sandcastle building to the enchanting world of snorkeling and coastal adventures, the Thai coastline provides a diverse range of activities for every traveler. Immerse yourself in the playful joy of crafting sand sculptures, explore the captivating underwater world through snorkeling, and embrace the thrill of coastal adventures that go beyond the beach. Your journey along Thailand's shores promises not only relaxation but also an exhilarating exploration of the natural wonders that make the country's beaches so iconic. So, pack your swimwear, your sense of adventure, and get ready to dive into the beach fun that Thailand has to offer.

6.3. Temples and Treasures: Cultural Expeditions for All

Thailand's rich cultural heritage is woven into its very fabric, from the ornate temples that dot the landscape to the vibrant markets and historical landmarks that tell tales of its past. In this chapter of our travel guidebook, we invite you to embark on a cultural expedition that will take you through Thailand's temples, markets, and historical sites. From the ancient grandeur of Ayutthaya to the bustling streets of Bangkok, these experiences offer a captivating glimpse into the country's diverse history and traditions.

Temple Marvels: Exploring Thailand's Spiritual Heritage:

Wat Phra Kaew and the Grand Palace, Bangkok:

Our journey begins at the heart of Thailand's capital, Bangkok. The Grand Palace, an architectural marvel, and Wat Phra Kaew, home to the revered Emerald Buddha, stand as icons of Thai culture and spirituality. Admire the intricate details of the buildings, the opulent decorations, and the serene atmosphere that envelops this sacred complex.

Wat Arun: The Temple of Dawn:

Located on the banks of the Chao Phraya River, Wat Arun's distinctive spires reach for the sky, creating an awe-inspiring sight that's especially magical during sunrise or sunset. Climb the steep steps of this temple to be rewarded with panoramic views of Bangkok's skyline and the river below.

Ayutthaya: Ancient Ruins and Historical Insights:

A journey to Ayutthaya, a UNESCO World Heritage Site, is a journey back in time. Explore the remnants of this once-mighty capital, where temples, palaces, and statues now stand as silent witnesses to its glorious past. Rent a bicycle to navigate the historical park and immerse yourself in the fascinating tales of Ayutthaya's rise and fall.

Local Markets: A Glimpse into Thai Life and Cuisine:

Damnoen Saduak Floating Market: Navigating the Waterways:

Experience the unique charm of Thailand's floating markets, where vendors ply their wares from traditional wooden boats. Damnoen Saduak Floating Market, located just outside Bangkok, offers a lively atmosphere and a chance to sample fresh fruits, local dishes, and artisanal crafts.

Chatuchak Weekend Market, Bangkok: A Shopper's Paradise:

One of the world's largest markets, Chatuchak Weekend Market, is a treasure trove of goods. From clothing and accessories to antiques and handicrafts, this bustling market presents an opportunity to interact with local vendors and uncover unique souvenirs.

Historical Landmarks: Tracing Thailand's Narrative:

Sukhothai Historical Park: Birthplace of Thai Civilization:

The Sukhothai Historical Park is another UNESCO World Heritage Site that provides a window into Thailand's past. The park is home to well-preserved ruins, including the iconic Buddha statues of Wat Si Chum. Cycling through the park's lush surroundings offers a serene exploration of ancient history.

Historic City of Chiang Mai:

The city of Chiang Mai is steeped in history, evident in its well-preserved temples and city walls. Visit Wat Phra Singh, home to the revered Phra Singh Buddha, and Wat Chedi Luang, where the massive chedi stands as a testament to the city's former glory.

Cultural Experiences: Embracing Thai Traditions:

Thai Cooking Classes: A Culinary Journey:

Engage your senses and learn the art of Thai cuisine through cooking classes. Explore local markets to select fresh ingredients, and then master the techniques to create classic dishes such as Pad Thai and Green Curry under the guidance of skilled instructors.

Traditional Thai Dance Performances: A Feast for the Senses:

Immerse yourself in the elegance of Thai culture through traditional dance performances. Witness intricate hand movements, vibrant costumes, and graceful choreography that tell stories of folklore, history, and mythology.

Thailand's cultural expeditions are a journey of discovery, offering insights into the country's past, present, and future. From the awe-inspiring temples that stand as architectural marvels to the bustling markets that reflect the vibrant soul of the nation, every step of the way is an opportunity to delve deeper into Thai culture. As you explore the historic landmarks, engage with local traditions, and savor the flavors of Thai cuisine, you'll find that every experience is a treasure that enriches your understanding of this captivating country. So, embrace the cultural diversity, immerse yourself in the heritage, and allow Thailand's temples and treasures to weave their magic as you embark on a truly transformative journey.

6.4. Hidden Gems

Thailand's allure extends far beyond its popular tourist destinations. Beyond the well-trodden paths lie hidden gems waiting to be discovered, offering a unique perspective of the country's diverse landscapes, culture, and traditions. In this chapter of our travel guidebook, we invite you to go off the beaten track and explore Thailand's lesser-known treasures. From secluded islands to charming villages and pristine natural wonders, these hidden gems promise unforgettable experiences that transcend the ordinary.

Koh Lanta: A Tranquil Island Retreat:

Koh Lanta's Beaches and Marine Life:

Nestled in the Andaman Sea, Koh Lanta is a serene haven that offers a peaceful escape from the crowds. Its pristine beaches, such as Klong Dao and Khlong Khong, boast soft sands and turquoise waters perfect for relaxation and snorkeling. The island's underwater world teems with colorful coral reefs and diverse marine life, making it a paradise for underwater enthusiasts.

Old Town's Cultural Charm:

Venture inland to Koh Lanta's Old Town, a historic enclave characterized by charming wooden houses and a unique blend of Thai, Chinese, and Muslim influences. Explore the quiet streets, boutique shops, and local eateries that reflect the island's multicultural heritage.

Pai: Bohemian Oasis in the Mountains:

Pai Canyon and Sunset Views:

Tucked away in the mountains of Northern Thailand, Pai exudes a laid-back atmosphere favored by backpackers and artists. Marvel at the Pai Canyon's narrow ridges, offering stunning panoramic views, particularly during sunrise and sunset.

Tha Pai Hot Springs and Pai River:

Indulge in the healing waters of Tha Pai Hot Springs, surrounded by lush greenery. For a serene experience, embark on a bamboo raft ride along the Pai River, offering glimpses of Pai's serene landscapes and local life.

Sukhothai: Ancient Ruins and Serenity:

Sukhothai Historical Park at Dawn:

While Sukhothai's historical significance is acknowledged, it remains a hidden gem compared to other UNESCO World Heritage Sites. Explore the Sukhothai Historical Park at sunrise to witness the ancient ruins bathed in soft morning light, creating a magical atmosphere.

Ramkhamhaeng National Park:

For nature lovers, Ramkhamhaeng National Park offers pristine landscapes, waterfalls, and opportunities for outdoor adventures like hiking and birdwatching.

Kanchanaburi: Nature's Beauty and Historical Reflections:

Erawan National Park: Seven-Tiered Waterfall:

Erawan National Park's multi-tiered waterfall, with its turquoise pools and lush surroundings, is a hidden gem of natural beauty. Trek through the jungle to reach each tier, taking refreshing dips along the way.

Hellfire Pass Memorial: Remembering History:

Delve into history at the Hellfire Pass Memorial, dedicated to the Allied prisoners of war and Asian laborers who built the Death Railway during World War II. The museum and walking trail offer poignant insights into the past.

Koh Mak: Secluded Island Paradise:

Koh Mak's Tranquil Beaches:

Escape to the tranquility of Koh Mak, a lesser-known island boasting unspoiled beaches and clear waters. Ao Kao Beach and Ao Suan Yai offer a secluded paradise for relaxation and snorkeling.

Exploring by Bicycle:

Rent a bicycle and explore the island at your own pace. Visit coconut plantations, fishing villages, and small resorts that reflect the island's idyllic charm.

Mae Hong Son: Hillside Haven:

Pai River: River Rafting and Exploration:

Mae Hong Son's natural beauty is best experienced along the Pai River. Embark on a river rafting adventure, navigating through lush landscapes and picturesque scenery.

Long Neck Karen Villages: Cultural Encounters:

Venture into the hills to visit the Long Neck Karen villages, where you can engage with local communities and learn about their unique customs and traditions.

Thailand's hidden gems are a testament to the country's diversity and enchantment. These lesser-known destinations offer a chance to connect with nature, immerse yourself in local culture, and discover the magic that lies beyond the tourist radar. As you journey through secluded islands, historical sites, and untouched landscapes, you'll find that these hidden gems provide a truly authentic and enriching travel experience. Embrace the sense of discovery, open your heart to new perspectives, and allow Thailand's hidden treasures to leave an indelible mark on your journey.

CHAPTER 7: Entertainment and Amusement

7.1. Theme Parks: Enjoyable Days at Dream World and Cartoon Network Amazone

Beyond its stunning natural landscapes and vibrant culture, Thailand offers a different kind of adventure for travelers seeking excitement and entertainment – theme parks. In this chapter of our travel guidebook, we invite you to step into the world of imagination and fun at two of Thailand's most popular theme parks: Dream World and Cartoon Network Amazon. From adrenaline-pumping rides to interactive attractions, these parks promise enjoyable days filled with laughter, thrills, and unforgettable memories.

Dream World: Where Fantasies Come to Life:

Adventure Land: Adrenaline Rush and Thrills:

Dream World's Adventure Land is a playground for thrill-seekers. Brace yourself for heart-pounding rides like the Tornado, a spinning roller coaster, and the Sky Coaster, which offers breathtaking views as you swing through the air. The Hurricane is another must-try, as it sends you soaring through loops and corkscrews at high speeds.

Fantasy Land: Whimsical Delights and Magic:

Step into the enchanting world of Fantasy Land, where fairy tales and classic stories come alive. The Sleeping Beauty Castle is a favorite among visitors, providing photo opportunities and a chance to explore charming exhibits. The Snow Town offers a unique experience with sub-zero temperatures, where you can build snowmen and enjoy snowball fights even in the tropical climate of Thailand.

Dream Garden: Tranquil Oasis and Relaxation:

For those seeking a serene escape, Dream Garden offers a peaceful respite from the excitement of the rides. Stroll through beautifully manicured gardens, enjoy boat rides on the lake, and relax by the colorful fountains. The garden's atmosphere provides a perfect balance to the high-energy attractions.

Hollywood Action: Silver Screen Adventures:

Immerse yourself in the glitz and glamor of Hollywood Action, where you can experience the thrill of being in an action movie. The Haunted Mansion takes visitors on a spooky journey through dark corridors and unexpected encounters, while the Super Splash guarantees a refreshing and splashing good time.

Cartoon Network Amazone: Cartoon Wonderland in Thailand:

Cartoonival Zone: Interactive Playgrounds:

Cartoon Network Amazone is a paradise for fans of beloved cartoon characters. The Cartoonival Zone is a colorful playground filled with interactive attractions, including the Adventure Time-themed Jake Jump, the Powerpuff Girls-themed Mojo Jojo's Robot Rampage, and the exciting Adventure Bay water play area.

Omniverse Zone: Thrilling Rides and Adventures:

The Omniverse Zone is home to the park's thrilling rides, including the Alien Attack roller coaster and the Ben 10 5D Hero Time experience. Feel the rush of adrenaline as you join your favorite characters on action-packed adventures.

Toon Machine: Family-Friendly Attractions:

Toon Machine offers attractions suitable for the whole family. From the family raft ride of Humunga Slide to the relaxing float of Goop Loop, these attractions provide opportunities for bonding and shared enjoyment.

Cartoon Network Entertainment: Shows and Meet-and-Greets:

Be sure to catch the live shows featuring beloved Cartoon Network characters. Join in the fun with dance performances, stage shows, and interactive games. Don't miss the chance to meet your favorite characters in person and capture memorable photos.

Thailand's theme parks, such as Dream World and Cartoon Network Amazon, offer a gateway to imagination, laughter, and endless fun. Whether you're seeking heart-pounding rides, interactive attractions, or family-friendly entertainment, these parks provide a diverse range of experiences for visitors of all ages. From the enchanting world of Dream World to the animated wonderland of Cartoon Network Amazon, every moment is a chance to create lasting memories and share unforgettable adventures with loved ones. So, gear up for a day of excitement, exploration, and entertainment, as you immerse yourself in the magic of Thailand's theme park experiences.

7.2. Thai Puppet Shows and Cultural Performances

Thailand's cultural heritage is a tapestry woven with vibrant traditions, artistic expressions, and captivating performances. In this chapter of our travel guidebook, we invite you to delve into the world of Thai puppet shows and cultural performances. These timeless art forms offer a window into the rich history, mythology, and storytelling that define Thai culture. From intricate puppetry to mesmerizing dance routines, these performances are an essential part of any traveler's journey to Thailand.

Thai Puppetry: Traditional Tales in Motion:

Traditional Khon Dance and Puppetry:

Khon, a classical Thai dance-drama, is often accompanied by intricately crafted puppets. These puppets, known as "Hun Lakorn Lek," are manipulated by skilled puppeteers who bring to life the epic tales of the Ramakien, Thailand's adaptation of the Indian Ramayana. The performances are a visual feast, featuring elaborate costumes, intricate hand movements, and rhythmic music that transport the audience to another era.

Joe Louis Puppet Theater: Contemporary Puppetry Delight:

The Joe Louis Puppet Theater in Bangkok is a modern take on traditional puppetry. Using an array of puppetry styles, including traditional hand puppets and larger-than-life puppets, the theater presents folktales, myths, and legends in an engaging and dynamic manner. The combination of traditional artistry and contemporary storytelling makes for a truly immersive experience.

Nang Yai: Shadow Puppetry with a Historical Twist:

Nang Yai, a form of shadow puppetry, is a visual spectacle that has been part of Thai culture for centuries. Intricate leather puppets are used to tell stories from ancient texts and history. The puppets are backlit, casting captivating shadows on a large white screen, creating a mesmerizing and ethereal effect that brings the narratives to life.

Cultural Performances: A Celebration of Heritage:

Traditional Thai Dance Performances:

Across Thailand, traditional dance performances celebrate the nation's cultural heritage. The elegant and graceful movements of dances like the "Fawn Thai" and the "Ram Wong" showcase the beauty of Thai aesthetics. Often performed at festivals and special occasions, these dances convey stories, emotions, and rituals that have been passed down through generations.

Thai Boxing (Muay Thai) Matches:

Muay Thai, the ancient martial art of Thailand, is not only a sport but also a cultural phenomenon.

Watching a Muay Thai match is an intense and riveting experience. The spectacle is not just about physical prowess but also embodies the values of discipline, respect, and honor deeply rooted in Thai culture.

Loy Krathong and Yi Peng Lantern Festivals:

These two annual festivals are celebrations of light and water, offering unique cultural performances. During Loy Krathong, people release floating lanterns onto rivers, symbolizing the release of negativity and making wishes. In Yi Peng, lanterns take to the skies, creating a breathtaking visual spectacle that transforms the night sky into a sea of twinkling lights.

Traditional Music and Instrument Performances:

Thai traditional music, with its melodic sounds and distinctive instruments like the "saw duang" and "ranat ek," is an integral part of Thai culture. You can enjoy live performances at cultural centers and events, where skilled musicians showcase the beauty of these traditional tunes.

Thai puppet shows and cultural performances are a testament to the country's artistic prowess, deep-rooted traditions, and storytelling heritage. These performances offer more than just entertainment; they provide insights into Thailand's past, beliefs, and values. Whether you're witnessing the graceful movements of traditional dance, the enchanting allure of shadow puppetry, or the captivating stories told through puppet shows, each performance offers a glimpse into the soul of Thailand. As you embrace these cultural experiences, you'll find yourself not just a spectator but a participant in the continuation of Thailand's artistic legacy, ensuring that these timeless traditions thrive for generations to come.

7.3. Family Boat Trips and Sunset Cruises for Couples

Thailand's stunning coastlines, turquoise waters, and picturesque islands offer the perfect backdrop for memorable boat trips and romantic sunset cruises. In this chapter of our travel guidebook, we invite families and couples alike to embark on journeys that combine relaxation, adventure, and breathtaking natural beauty. Whether you're seeking family-friendly activities or romantic moments, Thailand's waters provide a canvas for unforgettable experiences.

Family Boat Trips: Seafaring Adventures for All Ages:

Island-Hopping Adventures:

Embark on a family-friendly island-hopping adventure, exploring Thailand's pristine islands and their unique offerings. From the vibrant markets of Phi Phi Islands to the tranquil beaches of Koh Lanta, each island has its own charm and activities suitable for travelers of all ages.

Snorkeling and Marine Exploration:

Introduce your family to the wonders of the underwater world through snorkeling. Destinations like Koh Tao, Similan Islands, and Phang Nga Bay offer crystal-clear waters teeming with colorful marine life, creating opportunities for educational and immersive experiences.

James Bond Island Excursion:

Take your family on a journey to James Bond Island in Phang Nga Bay, made famous by the movie "The Man with the Golden Gun." Marvel at the dramatic limestone cliffs, explore hidden caves, and engage in fun activities like kayaking and swimming.

Sea Gypsy Villages and Cultural Insights:

Connect with local culture by visiting sea gypsy villages in regions like Phuket and Krabi. Engage in cultural exchanges, explore traditional stilt houses, and learn about the unique way of life of these coastal communities.

Sunset Cruises for Couples: Romance on the High Seas:

Andaman Sea Sunset Cruises:

Indulge in a romantic sunset cruise on the Andaman Sea. Board a traditional Thai longtail boat or a luxury yacht and set sail toward the horizon as the sun paints the sky with hues of orange and pink. Enjoy a private dinner on deck, accompanied by the gentle lapping of waves.

Chao Phraya River Romance:

Experience the romantic allure of Bangkok's Chao Phraya River on a sunset cruise. Glide past iconic landmarks, such as Wat Arun and the Grand Palace, as the city's lights twinkle against the fading daylight. The combination of historic sights and modern architecture creates a unique atmosphere.

Dinner Cruises and Thai Cuisine:

Treat your partner to a dinner cruise that not only offers breathtaking views but also a gastronomic journey through Thai cuisine. Savor delectable dishes as you cruise along the tranquil waters, surrounded by the enchanting ambiance of the night.

Private Charter for Intimate Moments:

For couples seeking utmost privacy and personalized experiences, consider chartering a private boat. Tailor the itinerary to your preferences, whether it's snorkeling, exploring hidden coves, or simply reveling in each other's company in a secluded paradise.

Family boat trips and sunset cruises for couples offer a range of experiences that showcase Thailand's natural beauty and cultural richness. From the thrill of island hopping and snorkeling with the family to the romantic allure of sunset cruises for couples, Thailand's waters provide the canvas for unforgettable memories. Whether you're seeking adventurous family outings or intimate moments under the setting sun, these boat trips offer a unique perspective of Thailand's coastal charm. As you sail on clear waters and witness breathtaking sunsets, you'll create lasting memories that celebrate the joy of togetherness and the beauty of nature's wonders.

CHAPTER 8: Practical Tips

8.1. Navigating Public Transportation with Ease

Thailand's vibrant cities, stunning landscapes, and rich culture make it an ideal destination for travelers seeking diverse experiences. To make the most of your journey, it's essential to familiarize yourself with the country's public transportation options. In this chapter of our travel guidebook, we provide you with comprehensive insights and tips to navigate public transportation in Thailand with ease, ensuring that your travels are convenient, efficient, and enjoyable.

The Benefits of Public Transportation:

Using public transportation in Thailand offers several advantages for travelers:

1. Cost-Effective: Public transportation is generally more budget-friendly than relying on taxis or private transfers, allowing you to save money for other experiences.

2. Eco-Friendly: Opting for public transportation reduces your carbon footprint and contributes to sustainable travel practices.

3. Cultural Immersion: Traveling alongside locals offers a chance to observe daily life, engage in cultural interactions, and gain a deeper understanding of the destination.

4. Traffic Avoidance: In bustling cities like Bangkok, public transportation can help you avoid traffic congestion and reach your destination more efficiently.

Modes of Public Transportation:

Skytrain (BTS) and Underground (MRT):

Bangkok's BTS Skytrain and MRT Underground are efficient and reliable options for navigating the city. The BTS covers both elevated and ground levels, while the MRT operates underground. Both systems connect key areas, major attractions, and shopping centers.

Tuk-Tuks:

Tuk-tuks are iconic three-wheeled vehicles that provide a quintessential Thai experience. Negotiate fares before boarding, and keep in mind that tuk-tuks may be more expensive than other options for the same distance.

Buses:

Thailand's cities have extensive bus networks, offering affordable travel options. Buses come in various types, including air-conditioned, non-air-conditioned, and express services. Research routes and schedules beforehand, as information may be available in Thai.

Songthaews:

Songthaews are shared pickup trucks or minivans that function as shared taxis. They are popular for short distances and can be flagged down on the street. Confirm the fare before boarding.

Ferries and Boats:

In coastal areas and islands, ferries and boats are common modes of transportation. These are essential for reaching destinations such as Phuket, Koh Samui, and Phi Phi Islands.

Trains:

Thailand's railway system connects major cities and regions. Trains offer a comfortable and scenic way to travel between destinations, with options ranging from sleeper trains to modern express services.

Motorbike Taxis:

Motorbike taxis are prevalent in urban areas, providing a quick and convenient way to navigate through traffic. Make sure to negotiate fares in advance.

Tips for Navigating Public Transportation:

1. Get a Transportation Card: In Bangkok, get a Rabbit card for the BTS and MRT or an Easy Card for buses and the MRT. These cards offer convenience and often discounted fares.

2. Use Mobile Apps: Download transportation apps like Grab (for ride-hailing services) and Google Maps for navigating routes and estimating travel times.

3. Learn Basic Phrases: While many signs are in English, learning basic Thai phrases for directions and fare inquiries can be helpful.

4. Plan Your Routes: Research routes and connections before heading out. Utilize online resources, maps, and apps to ensure a smooth journey.

5. Travel During Off-Peak Hours: Avoid rush hours, especially in major cities, to minimize crowds and congestion.

6. Have Small Change: Carry small denominations of Thai Baht for payment, especially on buses and songthaews.

Navigating public transportation in Thailand is a rewarding and integral part of your travel experience. From bustling city centers to serene islands, the country's diverse modes of transportation cater to various travel preferences and budgets. By familiarizing yourself with the available options, planning your routes, and embracing the local transportation culture, you'll not only enhance your journey but also connect with the heart and soul of Thailand's vibrant communities. So, hop on a tuk-tuk, board a ferry, or glide on a skytrain – let public transportation be your ticket to exploring the hidden gems and iconic landmarks that make Thailand a captivating destination.

8.2. Finding Child-Friendly Accommodations

Traveling with children is a rewarding experience that creates lasting memories and introduces them to new cultures and environments. To ensure a smooth and enjoyable family vacation in Thailand, choosing child-friendly accommodations is essential. In this chapter of our travel guidebook, we provide you with comprehensive insights and tips on finding the perfect accommodations that cater to the needs of both children and parents, making your stay in Thailand comfortable and memorable.

Considerations for Child-Friendly Accommodations:

Safety Measures:

Safety is paramount when traveling with children. Look for accommodations that offer childproofing measures such as outlet covers, corner guards, and stair gates. Ensure that balconies and windows are secure, and inquire about fire safety protocols.

Kid-Friendly Amenities:

Choose accommodations that provide amenities tailored to children's needs, such as baby cots, high chairs, baby baths, and changing tables. Some hotels and resorts also offer dedicated kids' pools, play areas, and supervised activities.

Location and Accessibility:

Opt for accommodations that are conveniently located near family-friendly attractions, parks, and restaurants. Proximity to public transportation and shopping centers can also enhance your convenience.

Room Configurations:

Check if the accommodations offer family suites, connecting rooms, or options with separate sleeping areas for children. Having the right room configuration can provide privacy for both parents and kids.

Recreational Facilities:

Look for accommodations with on-site recreational facilities such as pools, playgrounds, and game rooms. These amenities can keep children entertained during downtime.

Dining Options:

Accommodations that offer kid-friendly dining options, children's menus, and flexibility with meal times can make dining experiences more enjoyable for the whole family.

Childcare Services:

Some resorts and hotels offer childcare services, allowing parents to enjoy some alone time while knowing their children are in safe hands.

Family-Focused Activities:

Research accommodations that organize family-focused activities, workshops, and excursions to keep children engaged and create opportunities for family bonding.

Tips for Finding Child-Friendly Accommodations:

1. Research Online: Utilize travel websites, family travel blogs, and reviews from other parents to gather information about child-friendly accommodations in Thailand.

2. Contact the Hotel: Reach out to the hotel or resort directly to inquire about specific child-friendly amenities, services, and policies.

3. Ask for Recommendations: Seek recommendations from friends, family members, or online communities who have traveled to Thailand with children.

4. Read Reviews: Pay attention to reviews from families who have stayed at the accommodations. Their firsthand experiences can offer valuable insights.

5. Consider All-Inclusive Resorts: All-inclusive resorts often provide a variety of amenities, activities, and dining options that cater to families.

6. Prioritize Hygiene and Cleanliness: Cleanliness is crucial, especially when traveling with children. Read reviews and inquire about the accommodations' cleaning practices.

Finding child-friendly accommodations in Thailand is a crucial step to ensure a hassle-free and enjoyable family vacation. With careful consideration of safety measures, amenities, location, and services, you can select accommodations that cater to your family's needs and preferences. Whether you're exploring bustling cities, relaxing on pristine beaches, or immersing yourselves in cultural experiences, the right accommodations will enhance your family's journey and provide a comfortable home away from home. By planning ahead and selecting the right accommodations, you'll create cherished memories of your time in Thailand that your children will treasure for years to come.

8.3. Budgeting for a Memorable Trip

Embarking on a memorable trip to Thailand doesn't have to break the bank. With careful planning, smart choices, and a bit of financial discipline, you can experience the beauty, culture, and adventures of Thailand without compromising on the quality of your journey. In this chapter of our travel guidebook, we provide you with comprehensive insights and practical tips for budgeting effectively, making the most of your resources, and creating lasting memories during your visit to Thailand.

Setting a Realistic Budget:

Determine Your Travel Style:

Understand your travel preferences – whether you're a backpacker, a mid-range traveler, or someone seeking luxury experiences. Your travel style will influence your budget allocation for accommodations, dining, activities, and more.

Research Destination Costs:

Research the costs associated with your desired destinations in Thailand. Costs can vary significantly between cities, islands, and regions, so gather information to set accurate expectations.

Calculate Transportation Expenses:

Include costs for flights, local transportation (trains, buses, taxis), and any intercity travel. Booking flights and transportation in advance can help you secure better deals.

Estimate Accommodation Costs:

Research accommodation options within your budget range. Consider factors like location, amenities, and room types. Booking platforms often offer a variety of choices, from hostels to boutique hotels.

Factor in Meals and Dining:

Allocate a daily budget for meals and dining. Thailand's street food stalls and local eateries offer affordable and delicious options. You can save money by choosing local cuisine over international fare.

Plan Activities and Attractions:

List the activities and attractions you wish to experience in Thailand. Research entrance fees, tour costs, and activity expenses to budget accordingly.

Include Miscellaneous Expenses:

Budget for unforeseen expenses, souvenirs, tips, and incidentals. Having a cushion for unexpected costs ensures you're prepared for any situation.

Tips for Budgeting Effectively:

Prioritize Spending:

Allocate more budget to experiences that matter most to you. Prioritize activities, attractions, and accommodations that align with your interests and preferences.

Use a Budgeting App:

Utilize budgeting apps to track your expenses on-the-go. This will help you stay organized and ensure you're sticking to your budget.

Opt for Local Transportation:

Choose cost-effective transportation options like local buses, trains, and tuk-tuks instead of expensive taxis or private transfers.

Cook Meals Occasionally:

If your accommodation allows it, prepare simple meals or snacks to save on dining costs. This is particularly useful for families or longer stays.

Take Advantage of Free Activities:

Thailand offers numerous free or low-cost activities such as exploring markets, visiting temples, and enjoying nature hikes. Take advantage of these options to balance your budget.

Book in Advance:

Booking accommodations, flights, and tours in advance often yields better deals and discounts.

avel During Off-Peak Seasons:

Consider visiting Thailand during the shoulder seasons to take advantage of lower prices on accommodations and attractions.

Managing Your Finances:

Notify Your Bank:

Inform your bank about your travel dates to avoid any issues with using your credit or debit cards abroad.

Use Local Currency:

Use local currency (Thai Baht) for transactions to avoid unfavorable exchange rates and fees.

Carry Cash and Cards:

Have a mix of cash and cards for payment flexibility. Some places may only accept cash.

Budgeting for a memorable trip to Thailand is a strategic endeavor that allows you to make the most of your travel experience while managing your finances responsibly. By setting a realistic budget, researching destination costs, and making thoughtful spending choices, you can explore Thailand's cultural wonders, indulge in its cuisine, and embark on exciting adventures without undue financial stress. With careful planning and a focus on experiences that resonate with you, your journey to Thailand will not only be budget-friendly but also deeply enriching and unforgettable.

CHAPTER 9: Staying Healthy and Safe

9.1. Health Considerations and Vaccinations

When embarking on a journey to Thailand, it's essential to prioritize your health and well-being to ensure a safe and enjoyable travel experience. The vibrant culture, stunning landscapes, and mouthwatering cuisine are alluring, but being prepared for health considerations, including vaccinations, is crucial. This section of the travel guide aims to provide you with comprehensive information on health precautions and vaccinations to help you make informed decisions before your trip.

Health Considerations:

Travel Insurance:
Prior to your departure, securing comprehensive travel insurance is highly recommended. This insurance should cover medical expenses, emergency evacuation, trip cancellations, and other unforeseen events. Accidents and illnesses can happen anywhere, and having travel insurance will provide peace of mind throughout your journey.

Food and Water Safety:
While Thailand boasts a rich culinary scene, travelers should be cautious when it comes to food and water. Stick to bottled or boiled water, and avoid consuming raw or undercooked foods. Opt for meals from reputable restaurants and stalls that maintain proper hygiene practices.

Mosquito-Borne Diseases:
Thailand is located in a tropical region, making it prone to mosquito-borne diseases like dengue fever and malaria. Protect yourself by wearing long-sleeved clothing, using mosquito repellent, and staying in accommodations with proper screening and air conditioning.

Sun Protection:
The tropical sun can be intense, so pack and apply sunscreen with a high SPF regularly. Wear hats, sunglasses, and lightweight, breathable clothing to shield yourself from harmful UV rays.

Medical Facilities:
While major cities in Thailand offer modern medical facilities, remote areas may have limited healthcare resources. Familiarize yourself with the location of medical centers, clinics, and hospitals in

your vicinity and ensure you have access to their contact information.

Vaccinations:

Consulting a travel health specialist or your healthcare provider is crucial for determining which vaccinations you require based on your health history, itinerary, and current health recommendations. Below are some vaccinations that are commonly recommended for travelers to Thailand:

Routine Vaccinations:
Ensure that your routine vaccinations are up to date, including measles, mumps, rubella (MMR), diphtheria, tetanus, and pertussis (DTaP), polio, and influenza.

Hepatitis A and B:
Hepatitis A is prevalent in many parts of Thailand and can be contracted through contaminated food and water. Hepatitis B is a blood-borne disease that can be transmitted through various means, including unsafe medical procedures and sexual contact. Vaccination is advised for both.

Typhoid:

Typhoid fever can be contracted through contaminated food and water. Consider getting the typhoid vaccine, especially if you plan to explore rural areas.

Japanese Encephalitis:

This mosquito-borne disease is present in rural areas of Thailand. If you're spending a significant amount of time in these regions, particularly during the rainy season, consult your healthcare provider about the Japanese encephalitis vaccine.

Rabies:

If you plan to engage in activities that may expose you to animals, such as visiting wildlife reserves or volunteering with animals, consider getting the rabies vaccine. However, it's important to note that the vaccine doesn't eliminate the need for immediate medical attention if bitten by an animal.

Cholera:

While the risk of cholera is relatively low for most travelers, it's advisable to discuss with your healthcare provider whether the cholera vaccine is necessary based on your travel plans.

Prioritizing your health while traveling in Thailand is a key aspect of ensuring a memorable and enjoyable trip. Taking the necessary precautions, getting recommended vaccinations, and staying informed about potential health risks will contribute to a smoother and more worry-free travel experience. Remember that personal health circumstances and travel plans may vary, so consulting a healthcare professional is essential for tailoring your health preparations to your specific needs.

9.2. Sun Safety and Hydration Tips

Thailand's enchanting landscapes and vibrant culture draw travelers from all around the world, but its tropical climate can pose challenges for sun safety and staying hydrated. Whether you're exploring bustling markets, lounging on stunning beaches, or delving into the country's rich history, it's essential to prioritize sun protection and hydration to make the most of your journey. This section of the travel guide provides you with comprehensive insights into sun safety and hydration tips for your Thailand adventure.

Sun Safety:

Sunscreen Protection:

The Thai sun can be intense, especially during the peak hours of 10 am to 4 pm. Apply a broad-spectrum sunscreen with a high SPF (30 or above) to all exposed skin areas, including face, neck, ears, and hands. Reapply every two hours, or more frequently if swimming or sweating.

Protective Clothing:

Light, long-sleeved clothing made of breathable fabric offers excellent sun protection. Wearing a wide-brimmed hat and sunglasses with UV protection further shield your face and eyes from the sun's harmful rays.

Stay in the Shade:

Seek shade whenever possible, especially during the hottest parts of the day. Umbrellas, trees, and shaded areas can provide relief from direct sun exposure.

Hydrate Your Skin:

Use moisturizers and after-sun lotions to keep your skin hydrated and prevent sunburn-related dryness.

Heat-Reflective Surfaces:
Keep in mind that sand, water, and other reflective surfaces can intensify sun exposure. Be extra cautious in these environments.

Stay Hydrated:
Adequate hydration is paramount in a tropical climate. Dehydration can lead to fatigue, heat-related illnesses, and discomfort. Carry a reusable water bottle and drink water regularly throughout the day, even if you don't feel thirsty.

Hydration Tips:

Drink Clean Water:
Opt for bottled water or purified water from reputable sources. Avoid tap water and ice in drinks, as they might not meet the same standards of cleanliness as you're accustomed to.

Hydrating Foods:
Consume fruits and vegetables with high water content, such as watermelon, cucumbers, and oranges. These foods help replenish fluids and provide essential vitamins and minerals.

Electrolytes:

Sweating in Thailand's heat can lead to the loss of electrolytes. Consider drinking electrolyte-rich beverages or consuming electrolyte tablets to maintain a proper balance.

Limit Alcohol and Caffeine:

Alcohol and caffeine can contribute to dehydration. While enjoying Thailand's nightlife and flavorful drinks, be mindful of your alcohol and caffeine intake, and alternate with water.

Monitor Urine Color:

An easy way to gauge your hydration level is by checking the color of your urine. Pale yellow or straw-colored urine indicates proper hydration, while dark yellow or amber suggests you need to drink more fluids.

Rehydrate After Activities:

Engaging in outdoor activities, such as hiking or sightseeing, can lead to increased fluid loss. Rehydrate after such activities to prevent dehydration.

Thailand's tropical climate adds to its allure, but it's important to respect the sun's power and the challenges it presents. By following sun safety practices and staying properly hydrated, you'll not only protect your health but also ensure a more enjoyable and comfortable journey. Prepare by packing sunscreen, protective clothing, and a refillable water bottle, and make conscious efforts to maintain your hydration throughout your Thai adventure. Your well-being is key to fully immersing yourself in the beauty and culture of this captivating destination.

9.3. Emergency Contacts and Medical Facilities

Exploring the vibrant culture and breathtaking landscapes of Thailand is a thrilling experience, but it's essential to be prepared for any unforeseen circumstances that may arise during your travels. Familiarizing yourself with emergency contacts and understanding the healthcare system can make all the difference in ensuring your safety and well-being. This section of the travel guide provides in-depth insights into emergency contacts and medical facilities in Thailand, empowering you to navigate potential challenges with confidence.

Emergency Contacts:

Tourist Police:

The Tourist Police in Thailand are specifically trained to assist travelers. They can provide guidance, help in case of lost belongings, and offer assistance in emergency situations. Their contact number is 1155, and they often have English-speaking officers.

Police:

In case of any criminal incident or emergency, you can dial the national police emergency number, 191. While English-speaking officers may be available in major tourist areas, it's advisable to have a Thai-speaking local assist you in communicating with the police.

Ambulance and Medical Emergencies:

For medical emergencies, including accidents or serious illnesses, dial 1669 for an ambulance. English-speaking operators might be available, but it's helpful to have a local guide or someone who speaks Thai assist you.

Fire Department:

In the event of a fire or related emergencies, dial 199.

Embassy Contacts:

Contact information for your country's embassy or consulate in Thailand should be kept readily available. They can provide assistance with passport replacement, legal matters, and emergency situations involving citizens of your home country.

Local Contacts:
Store the contact information of your accommodation, local guide, or any friends you make during your trip. They can provide assistance or connect you with the appropriate authorities if needed.

Medical Facilities:

Hospitals and Clinics:
Thailand boasts a range of medical facilities, from modern hospitals in urban areas to smaller clinics in rural regions. In major cities like Bangkok and Chiang Mai, you'll find internationally accredited hospitals with English-speaking staff. Bumrungrad International Hospital in Bangkok is renowned for its medical services.

Pharmacies:
Pharmacies (known as "drug stores" locally) are widespread in Thailand. You can purchase

over-the-counter medications and basic medical supplies. For prescription medications or specialized treatments, consult a doctor.

Health Insurance:

It's imperative to have comprehensive travel health insurance that covers medical expenses, emergency evacuation, and repatriation. Confirm that your insurance policy is accepted by the medical facilities you might visit.

Language Barrier:

While medical professionals in major tourist areas often speak English, it's advisable to have a basic translation app or phrasebook to facilitate communication in case of language barriers.

Medications and Prescriptions:

If you're bringing prescription medications, ensure you have enough for the duration of your stay. Carry a copy of your prescriptions and a note from your doctor explaining your medical condition and required medications.

Traveler's Tips:

Research Beforehand:

Before your trip, research the medical facilities available in the areas you plan to visit. Know where the nearest hospitals, clinics, and pharmacies are located.

Keep Documentation:
Keep a copy of important documents, including your passport, insurance policy, and emergency contacts, in a safe place. Consider having digital copies accessible on your phone or cloud storage.

Notify Loved Ones:
Inform friends or family members about your travel plans and provide them with your itinerary and contact information for your accommodations.

Emergency Funds:
Have access to emergency funds that can cover unexpected medical expenses or unforeseen situations.

Local Guidance:
In case of medical emergencies, local residents or your accommodation staff can provide guidance and assistance in seeking appropriate medical care.

Thailand's enchanting landscapes and vibrant culture make for an unforgettable journey, but being prepared for emergencies is paramount. By understanding emergency contacts, medical facilities, and relevant protocols, you can navigate any challenges that may arise with confidence. Prioritize your safety and well-being by staying informed, having comprehensive travel insurance, and taking precautions to ensure a smooth and secure travel experience in the Land of Smiles.

CHAPTER 10: Capturing Memories

10.1. Photography Tips for Family and Couple Travel

Embarking on a family or couple's adventure in the captivating landscapes of Thailand offers a plethora of picturesque opportunities. From stunning beaches and lush jungles to vibrant cities and ancient temples, Thailand presents a photographer's paradise. This section of the travel guide aims to provide comprehensive photography tips to help you capture cherished moments while exploring the magical beauty of Thailand.

Research and Plan Ahead:
Before setting off on your journey, conduct thorough research on the destinations you'll be visiting. Familiarize yourself with the iconic landmarks, local culture, and natural beauty of each location. This knowledge will guide your photography choices and help you anticipate ideal shooting times and lighting conditions.

Pack the Right Gear:
When packing your photography equipment, consider the versatility of your gear. A lightweight and high-quality DSLR or mirrorless camera with interchangeable lenses is recommended. A

wide-angle lens can capture breathtaking landscapes, while a portrait lens can beautifully highlight the emotions of your loved ones.

Golden Hours are Golden:
Thailand's warm and soft lighting during the golden hours – shortly after sunrise and before sunset – provides the perfect backdrop for intimate family and couple photographs. The soft light enhances colors, reduces harsh shadows, and adds a magical touch to your images.

Embrace the Local Culture:
Immerse yourself in Thailand's rich cultural tapestry. Engage with locals and ask for permission before taking their photographs. Respect sacred spaces like temples and be mindful of local customs. These interactions can lead to authentic and heartwarming shots that tell the story of your journey.

Capture Candid Moments:
Some of the most precious memories unfold naturally. Candid shots capture genuine emotions and interactions. Photograph your loved ones as they explore local markets, enjoy a tuk-tuk ride, or simply revel in the beauty around them.

Explore Unique Perspectives:

Experiment with different angles and perspectives to create dynamic and eye-catching images. Capture your family from above as they walk along a pier or photograph a couple silhouetted against a vibrant sunset. Don't be afraid to get creative!

Utilize Leading Lines:

Thailand's landscapes often feature natural leading lines – pathways, rivers, or streets – that draw the viewer's eye into the frame. Incorporate these lines into your composition to add depth and guide attention to your subjects.

Balance and Symmetry:

Thailand's temples and architecture are known for their intricate designs and symmetrical structures. Utilize symmetry and balance to create visually striking images. Frame your family or couple at the center of a symmetrical scene, such as a temple courtyard or a row of market stalls.

Incorporate Nature:

Thailand's lush natural beauty is an asset to your photography. Whether it's the crystal-clear waters of the Andaman Sea, the dense jungles of Chiang Mai, or the serene rice terraces, make nature an integral part of your shots.

Editing for Perfection:

Post-processing plays a crucial role in enhancing your photographs. Use editing software to adjust exposure, contrast, and colors. Avoid over-processing, striving for a natural look that reflects the authentic atmosphere of your experiences.

Documenting Food Adventures:

Thai cuisine is renowned worldwide for its flavors and presentation. Capture the essence of your culinary journey by photographing dishes against vibrant markets or authentic street food stalls. Experiment with close-up shots to showcase the intricate details.

Cherish Unfiltered Moments:

While it's important to aim for visually appealing shots, remember that genuine moments often hold the most significance. Candid laughter, stolen glances, and shared experiences are the heart of your family or couple's travel adventure.

Thailand's diverse landscapes, rich culture, and warm atmosphere create an ideal canvas for capturing memorable family and couple moments. By planning ahead, embracing local culture, and employing various photography techniques, you can create a vibrant and heartfelt visual narrative of your journey through this enchanting destination. So, pack your gear, embrace the beauty of Thailand, and capture the moments that will become cherished memories for years to come.

CHAPTER 11: Making the Most of Your Trip

11.1. Balancing Family and Couple Time

Thailand, with its captivating landscapes, rich culture, and diverse experiences, offers an idyllic setting for both family adventures and romantic getaways. This section of the travel guide delves into the art of balancing family and couple time during your stay in Thailand. By finding harmony between quality time with your loved ones and intimate moments with your partner, you can create a memorable and well-rounded vacation experience.

Setting Expectations:
Begin your journey by openly communicating with both your family and your partner about your travel expectations. Discuss activities that each group is excited about and create a flexible itinerary that accommodates everyone's interests.

Finding Common Ground:
Identify activities and destinations that can be enjoyed by both family members and couples. Beach days, cultural excursions, and leisurely strolls through bustling markets are examples of experiences that can be relished by all.

Allocate Dedicated Time:
Designate specific blocks of time for family activities and couple moments. This ensures that both groups have their share of quality time without feeling neglected.

Family-Friendly Destinations:
Explore family-friendly destinations like the islands of Phuket or Koh Samui. These areas offer a mix of child-friendly attractions, such as water parks and animal sanctuaries, as well as serene beaches for couples to unwind.

Group-Friendly Experiences:
Engage in activities that accommodate both family and couple dynamics. Consider taking a Thai cooking class where everyone can participate, or embark on a boat tour that combines relaxation and exploration.

Mini Escapes:

Plan for short, supervised breaks for couples while the family engages in kid-friendly activities. Utilize this time to explore a nearby café, stroll along the beach, or indulge in a spa treatment.

Kids' Clubs and Childcare:

Many resorts and hotels in Thailand offer kids' clubs or childcare services. Take advantage of these facilities to give both parents and couples some quality time for relaxation and exploration.

Sunset Rituals:

Witnessing the breathtaking sunsets that grace Thailand's horizons is an experience that can be enjoyed by all. Capture these magical moments as a family, and then later, share an intimate sunset viewing with your partner.

Exploring Night Markets:

Night markets are a wonderful fusion of shopping, dining, and cultural immersion. Spend a family evening exploring stalls and trying local delicacies, and later, return with your partner for a more romantic stroll.

Balancing Excursions:

Choose excursions that cater to various interests. While families may enjoy visits to zoos or theme parks, couples might prefer temple visits or serene boat rides through mangroves.

Open Dialogue:
Regularly check in with both your family and your partner to ensure everyone feels valued and heard. Adjust the itinerary as needed to address any concerns or desires that arise during the trip.

Capturing Shared Memories:
Document both family and couple moments through photography. Create a visual diary that showcases the bond you share with your family and the intimacy you experience with your partner.

Finding equilibrium between family and couple time during your stay in Thailand is a delicate yet rewarding endeavor. By fostering open communication, seeking common experiences, and carefully planning your itinerary, you can create a vacation that caters to the diverse needs and desires of everyone involved. Embrace the joy of togetherness with your family, and savor the romantic moments that unfold between you and your partner in this enchanting destination.

11.2. Embracing Spontaneity: Hidden Gems and Unexpected Adventures

While planning a trip is essential, leaving room for spontaneity can lead to some of the most memorable and enchanting experiences. Thailand, with its vibrant culture, diverse landscapes, and warm hospitality, offers countless hidden gems and unexpected adventures waiting to be discovered. This section of the travel guide encourages you to step off the beaten path, embrace spontaneity, and uncover the lesser-known wonders that Thailand has to offer.

Open-Minded Exploration:
Approach your journey with an open mind and a willingness to deviate from your itinerary. Allow yourself to be guided by curiosity and the allure of the unknown.

Local Recommendations:
Engage with locals and seek their recommendations for off-the-beaten-path destinations. Locals often know about the best-kept secrets that are not mentioned in guidebooks.

Serendipitous Wanderings:
Take leisurely strolls through neighborhoods and markets. Serendipitous encounters with interesting

shops, unique street art, and friendly locals can lead to delightful adventures.

Chasing Cultural Festivals:
Thailand is known for its vibrant festivals, many of which are celebrated spontaneously. Keep an ear out for local events such as lantern festivals, temple fairs, and traditional ceremonies.

Exploring Backstreets:
Venture beyond the main streets and explore the narrow alleys and backstreets of towns and cities. These areas often reveal charming cafes, hidden shrines, and authentic glimpses of local life.

Island Hopping Off the Beaten Path:
While popular islands like Phuket and Koh Phi Phi are well-known, consider visiting lesser-known islands like Koh Lanta, Koh Lipe, or Koh Tao for a more secluded and intimate island experience.

Trekking in Remote Villages:
Explore the lush countryside by embarking on a trek through remote villages. This not only offers a chance to appreciate Thailand's natural beauty but also to connect with local communities.

Homestays and Eco-Lodges:

Opt for accommodations that offer a more immersive experience, such as homestays or eco-lodges. These provide opportunities to interact with locals and explore hidden corners of the region.

Unplanned Culinary Adventures:
Let your taste buds guide you to unassuming street food stalls and local eateries. Trying unexpected dishes can be a culinary adventure in itself.

Impromptu Beach Picnics:
Pack a picnic and head to a secluded beach. Serene shores offer the perfect backdrop for spontaneous moments of relaxation and bonding.

Unforeseen Encounters with Wildlife:
Thailand's natural landscapes are home to diverse wildlife. Be prepared for chance encounters with monkeys, tropical birds, and even elephants in unexpected locations.

Random Cultural Workshops:
Enroll in impromptu workshops or classes that offer hands-on experiences with traditional Thai crafts, such as fruit carving, batik painting, or Thai boxing.

Documenting the Unplanned:
Keep a travel journal or a digital diary to document your spontaneous experiences. Record the emotions, sights, and sounds that make these moments truly unique.

Thailand's allure lies not only in its well-known attractions but also in the hidden gems and unexpected adventures that await those who are willing to embrace spontaneity. By relinquishing strict schedules and allowing yourself to be guided by your instincts, you open the door to a world of serendipitous discoveries and genuine interactions. These unplanned moments have the power to create lasting memories that capture the true essence of Thailand's beauty, culture, and people. So, venture off the beaten path, immerse yourself in the unexpected, and let Thailand's hidden wonders unfold before your eyes.

11.3. Language Guide: Basic Thai Phrases

One of the most enriching aspects of travel is immersing oneself in the local culture, and language plays a vital role in this endeavor. While English is widely spoken in popular tourist areas of Thailand, learning a few basic Thai phrases can greatly enhance your interactions and leave a positive impression on locals. This language guide section of the travel book will provide you with essential Thai phrases to help you navigate daily situations, connect with locals, and make the most of your journey.

Greetings and Polite Expressions:
- Hello: สวัสดี (sawasdee)
- Goodbye: ลาก่อน (laa gòn)
- Thank you: ขอบคุณ (kòp khun)
- Yes: ใช่ (châi)
- No: ไม่ (mâi)

Basic Conversation:
- How are you?: สบายดีไหม (sà-baai dee mái)
- I'm fine, thank you: สบายดีครับ/ค่ะ (sà-baai dee kráp/kâ)
- What is your name?: คุณชื่ออะไร (khun chûe à-rai)
- My name is [your name]: ฉันชื่อ [your name] (chăn chûe [your name])

Asking for Help:
- Excuse me: ขอโทษ (kŏr tôht)
- I'm lost: ฉันหลงทาง (chăn lŏng tāang)
- Can you help me?: คุณช่วยหน่อยได้ไหม (khun chûay nòi dâi mái)

Ordering Food:

- I would like [dish]: ฉันต้องการ [dish] (chăn dtâwng gaan [dish])
- How much is this?: นี่ราคาเท่าไหร่ (nîi raa-kăa tâo-rài)
- Delicious: อร่อย (à-ràu-ay)

Getting Around:
- Where is [place]?: [place] อยู่ที่ไหน ([place] yùu tîi năi)
- How do I get to [place]?: จะไป [place] ยังไง (jà bpai [place] yang-ngai)

Shopping and Bargaining:
- How much does this cost?: นี่ราคาเท่าไหร่ (nîi raa-kăa tâo-rài)
- Can you give me a discount?: ลดราคาได้ไหม (lót raa-kăa dâi mái)

Emergency Phrases:
- Help!: ช่วยด้วย (chûay dûay)
- I need a doctor: ฉันต้องการหมอ (chăn dtâwng gaan mŏr)

Expressing Gratitude:
- You're welcome: ยินดี (yin dee)
- I appreciate it: ขอบคุณมาก (kòp khun mâak)

Numbers:

- 1: หนึ่ง (nèung)
- 2: สอง (sŏng)
- 3: สาม (săam)
- 4: สี่ (sìi)
- 5: ห้า (hâa)
- 10: สิบ (sìp)

Learning a few basic Thai phrases can go a long way in enhancing your travel experience in Thailand. Locals will appreciate your effort to connect through their language, and your interactions will become more meaningful and enjoyable. Even if you're not fluent, a few well-placed words can lead to laughter, connections, and unforgettable memories. So, practice these essential phrases, engage with locals, and open the door to a more immersive and rewarding adventure in the Land of Smiles.

11.4. Saying Goodbye to Thailand: Souvenirs and Fond Farewells

As your journey in Thailand comes to an end, it's time to bid farewell to the captivating landscapes, vibrant culture, and warm hospitality that have embraced you throughout your stay. This section of the travel guide focuses on how to commemorate your time in Thailand through meaningful souvenirs and heartfelt farewells. By carefully selecting keepsakes and expressing your gratitude to the people you've encountered, you can carry a piece of Thailand's magic with you as you embark on your next adventure.

Souvenir Selection:

Cultural Treasures:
Look for authentic crafts and art that reflect Thailand's rich heritage. Handmade textiles, intricate wood carvings, and traditional ceramics are not only beautiful but also carry the essence of the country's culture.

Natural Reminders:
Thailand's stunning landscapes inspire a range of nature-inspired souvenirs. Consider gemstone jewelry, silk scarves with floral motifs, or aromatic oils made from local herbs.

Culinary Delights:
Spices, teas, and sauces unique to Thai cuisine make for flavorful souvenirs. Packaged in beautifully designed containers, they serve as a reminder of the gastronomic delights you enjoyed.

Ethical Souvenir Shopping:

Support Local Artisans:
Seek out markets and boutiques that support local craftsmen and artists. Purchasing directly from artisans ensures that your souvenirs have a positive impact on the communities you've visited.

Sustainable Choices:
Opt for products made from sustainable materials or those that promote environmental conservation. Bamboo products, eco-friendly textiles, and organic skincare are excellent options.

Fair Trade Initiatives:
Look for souvenirs that are part of fair trade initiatives, ensuring that the creators receive fair compensation for their work.

Heartfelt Farewells:

Thanking Local Friends:
If you've formed connections with locals, express your gratitude with a heartfelt thank-you note or a small gift. This gesture demonstrates your appreciation for the warmth and kindness you've experienced.

Hotel and Service Staff:
Take a moment to thank the staff at your accommodations or those who have provided exceptional service. A kind word or a small tip can make a lasting impact.

Sharing Memories:
Capture your fondest memories in photographs and share them with the people you've met. This not only reinforces the bonds you've formed but also leaves behind a piece of your journey.

Creating Lasting Memories:

Journaling:
Maintain a travel journal where you jot down daily reflections, experiences, and interactions. This personalized keepsake will transport you back to your time in Thailand whenever you revisit its pages.

Photography:
Take ample photos of the places, people, and moments that have touched your heart. Create a photo album or digital gallery that immortalizes your Thai adventure.

Planning a Return:
As you bid farewell to Thailand, consider planning a return trip in the future. The anticipation of revisiting cherished places and reconnecting with familiar faces can be a beautiful way to say "see you later."

Saying goodbye to Thailand doesn't have to mean leaving it all behind. Through thoughtfully chosen souvenirs and sincere farewells, you can carry the essence of your journey with you. These tokens of your adventure, combined with the connections you've made, will serve as lasting reminders of the beauty, culture, and kindness that Thailand bestowed upon you. As you embark on new horizons, remember that the memories you've created are forever intertwined with the tapestry of your life's journey.

Printed in Great Britain
by Amazon

33555708R00090